The Fast-Track MI

Co-published with AMED (the Association for Management Education and Development)

Consultant Editors
John Kind, Director, Harbridge Consulting Group
David Megginson, Associate Head, Sheffield Business School

THE FAST-TRACK MBA SERIES represents an innovative and refreshingly different approach to presenting core subjects in a typical MBA syllabus in a lively and accessible way. The usual text book approach is eschewed in favour of a practical, action-oriented style which involves the reader in self-assessment and participation.

Ideal for managers wanting to renew or develop their management capabilities, the books in *THE FAST-TRACK MBA SERIES* rapidly give readers a sound knowledge of all aspects of business and management that will boost both self-confidence and career prospects. For those fortunate enough to take an MBA, the *Series* will provide a solid grounding in the subjects to be studied. Managers and students worldwide will find this new series an exciting and challenging alternative to the usual study texts and management guides.

Titles already available in the series are:

★ *Strategic Management* (Robert Grant & James Craig)
★ *Organisational Behaviour and Design* (Barry Cushway & Derek Lodge)
★ *Problem Solving and Decision Making* (Graham Wilson)
★ *Human Resource Development* (David Megginson, Jennifer Joy-Matthews & Paul Banfield)

Forthcoming books in the series will cover:

Accounting ★ Data Analysis and IT ★ Financial Management ★ Human Resource Management ★ International Management ★ Investment and Risk ★ Law ★ Business Ethics ★ Economics ★ Marketing ★ Operations Management.

AMED is an association of individuals who have a professional interest in the development of people at work. AMED's network brings together people from industry, the public sector, academic organizations and consultancy, and is exclusive to individuals.

The aims of AMED are to promote best practice in the fields of individual and organizational development, to provide a forum for the exploration of new ideas, to offer members opportunities for their own development and to encourage the adoption of ethical practices in development.

For further information on AMED you are invited to write to AMED, 21 Catherine Street, London WC2B 5JS.

Organisational Behaviour and Design

BARRY CUSHWAY

DEREK LODGE

Published in association with  AMED

KOGAN
PAGE

First published in 1993

Kogan Page Limited
120 Pentonville Road
London N1 9JN

British Library Cataloguing in Publication Data

A CIP record for this book is available from the British Library.

ISBN 0 7494 1148 1

Typeset by Saxon Graphics Ltd, Derby
Printed in England by Clays Ltd, St Ives plc.

Contents

Acknowledgements

Our main emphasis in this book has been on producing something that will be of practical application. It therefore draws heavily on our experience of how things actually work in organisations and of the practical approaches used to analyse and resolve organisational problems. We have tried to keep theory to the minimum necessary to gain a sound understanding of the area.

Much of the credit for the thinking behind the approaches described in this book must go to the various organisations we have worked for. In particular this includes MSL Human Resources Consulting, Hay Management Consultants and Price Waterhouse. Naturally, as time has gone by we have applied, refined and developed (consciously and unconsciously) all we have learnt from these and other sources. These sources, in turn, have no doubt drawn from ideas originally developed elsewhere. Inevitably this means that in many cases the origins of our received wisdom are obscure and we therefore apologise for any failure to attribute credit where it is due.

Specific thanks are owed to Dr Robert Edenborough of MSL for his contribution on the application of psychometric testing and assessment and development centres, to Pam West for doing the bulk of the typing and turning it round so quickly and to the assistance received from Sheelagh McCrea and Kiki Peros at MSL. Thanks are also owed to our families for their tolerance of all those little jobs that still need doing.

Finally, we would like to thank all those publishers and other organisations that have given us permission to reproduce or quote extracts from various sources.

Barry Cushway
Derek Lodge
August 1993

An Introduction to Organisational Behaviour and Design

THE MEANING OF ORGANISATIONAL BEHAVIOUR

The term 'organisational behaviour', as used in this book, refers to the way in which individuals and groups act in the organisation and the influences on these actions and behaviour patterns. It takes account of people's attitudes and beliefs and tries to examine some of the reasons for them. The overall emphasis, however, is on the impact of, on the one hand, individual and group behaviour on the organisation and, on the other, the organisation's impact on that same behaviour.

THE MEANING OF ORGANISATIONAL DESIGN

The term 'organisational design' refers to the different parts of the organisation and the separate elements that are brought together to create it, and considers both how these fit together and ways in which they may be analysed and improved. The design aspects include how the organisation is structured, the types and numbers of jobs, and the processes and procedures used to:

- handle and pass information;
- make decisions;
- produce results;
- manage quality;
- communicate information;
- plan, develop and manage resources;
- innovate and handle crises.

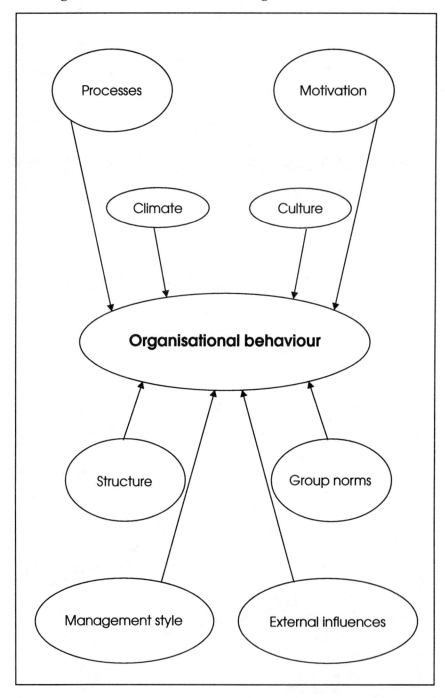

Figure 1.1 *Some influences on organisational behaviour*

THE MAIN INFLUENCES ON ORGANISATIONAL BEHAVIOUR

Some of the main influences on organisational behaviour are summarised in Figure 1.1. However, you should note that it is not a one-way process. While all the factors shown will influence how people behave at work, people's behaviour will in turn often have an effect on those factors. This is more true of some than others. For example, an individual may have little influence on the organisation's formal structure (although the same person could have a significant effect on the informal structure, as explained below), while the organisation's climate depends significantly on employees' attitudes and behaviour. Each of these factors is considered in more detail below.

Organisation climate

The organisation's climate originates in the feelings and emotions of the employees and encompasses what it feels like to work for the organisation. This in turn will affect motivation and behaviour in the organisation.

Organisation culture

The culture can be seen as the values and beliefs that are central to the organisation. This is the core philosophy that drives the organisation and it may have developed over a long period of time.

Motivation

Motivation refers to the drives which affect individual behaviour within the organisation and the degree of commitment shown by employees to the achievement of goals and objectives.

Group norms

Group norms are the values and standards established by particular groups within the organisation. Employees may be members of such groups or be influenced by them. Work groups that people belong to can have a particularly strong influence over the way they behave in the workplace; for example, they may have a say in how hard an individual works when there is a group or team productivity bonus being paid.

External influences

External influences include all the pressures on people that can affect behaviour in the workplace. These can include their family circumstances, membership of organisations, social background and so on.

Management style

Management style refers to the habitual way in which managers run the organisation. This may, at one extreme, be very authoritarian, requiring people to obey orders without question; or it may be highly democratic, every decision being discussed widely with employees before being finalised.

Organisation structure

Structure refers to the way the organisation is organised and, in particular, to the grouping of functions and lines of communication and control. This formal structure lays down who has the authority to make decisions and to whom individuals report. The informal structure, on the other hand, is what happens in practice. For example, individuals may sometimes bypass the person they are supposed to report to, or a manager may sometimes go straight to a particular employee, ignoring his or her supervisor.

Processes

Processes are all the systems of the organisation which ensure that its activities are successfully undertaken. Most organisations would generally need to have systems for maintaining the organisation on a day-to-day basis, for adapting to change and new developments, and for handling crises.

THE ORGANISATION AS A SYSTEM

The organisation can generally be regarded as an open system. This means in effect that it is a set of activities which have a common purpose and for which there are outputs and inputs. The outputs will generally be products and services, while the inputs will be raw materials, money, people and so on. Within the organisation there will be subsystems for managing strategy, operations, and the support structure and processes. A simplified diagram showing some of the major influences on the organisation's outputs is shown in Figure 1.2.

Any organisation is dynamic and will be affected to a greater or lesser extent by changes in the external environment. For example,

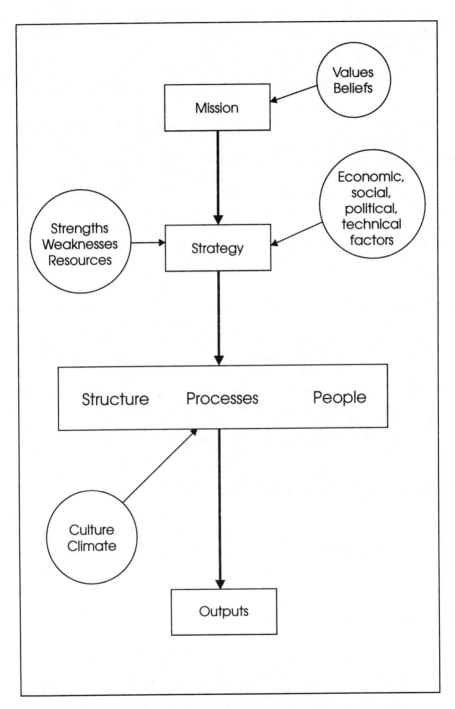

Figure 1.2   *Major influences on organisational outputs*

changes to the economy will affect business performance and changes in legislation will have an impact on the way organisations operate.

THE STRUCTURE OF THIS BOOK

What has been said above is relevant to the structure of this book. While each subject has been considered separately, this is for convenience only, as they are all interrelated. For example, the way the organisation is structured will affect jobs and roles, and the way these are carried out will in turn have an impact on motivation. However, the general approach has been to separate the behavioural elements from the more structural ones.

The general themes of each chapter are as follows.

Chapter 2 — Classification of organisations

While it is in many ways rather difficult to put complex and irregularly shaped entities such as organisations into neatly pro-portioned boxes, it is sometimes necessary to try to do so in order to make comparisons between them. For example, an organisation providing services to a range of companies will find that for marketing purposes it will be necessary to group those companies together in some way. Similarly, if comparisons are to be made regarding performance, or the salary of the chief executive, it will be necessary to categorise organisations by size and type. This chapter reviews some of the main approaches to such classification.

Chapter 3 — Organisational analysis

Being able to analyse organisations can be important in determin-ing whether they are working as effectively as they could be, and what improvements might be necessary. Different ways of analysing organisations and the people within them are considered in this chapter.

Chapter 4 — Mission and strategy

This chapter describes what is meant by an organisation's mission, what it should look like and how it should be prepared. It also shows how to develop strategic objectives and define critical success factors. The importance of these elements to the organisa-tion is also discussed.

Chapter 5 — Organisation, design and structure

This chapter describes the importance of the organisation's structure and how it can be analysed and modified. It reviews a number of different types of structure together with their advantages and disadvantages, and examines some of the typical problems.

Chapter 6 — Jobs and roles

This chapter explains how jobs can be designed, changed and analysed. It also discusses the concept of roles in the organisation and the impact they can have on job satisfaction. The importance of effective job design is also considered.

Chapter 7 — Teams and groups

This chapter describes the importance of teams and groups and their influence on people within the organisation. It also examines the effectiveness of group decision making and describes the concept of empowerment.

Chapter 8 — Motivation and reward

This chapter describes what motivates employees and considers a number of the major theories in this area. An understanding of the theory of motivation is an important background to many of today's reward policies and is an essential starting point for any discussion on this topic. The chapter also considers the different kinds of rewards available and describes alternative approaches.

Chapter 9 — The management role

This discusses in some detail the role of managers, with particular reference to leadership and different management styles. It underlines the importance of the management role in the organisation, and the effect different styles can have on motivation and performance.

Chapter 10 — Communication

This chapter describes what is meant by communication and the various barriers to effective communication. It also considers techniques for improving communication in the organisation.

2

Classification of Organisations

THE COMMON ELEMENTS IN ORGANISATIONS

All manner of organisations exist and there is, on the face of it, little similarity between, say, a golf club and a manufacturing firm. However, it is important to be able to compare organisations, if for no other reason than to separate the relatively good performers from the relatively poor ones. Obviously this kind of judgement is important when it comes to making investment (or career) decisions.

Despite the variations, all organisations do have certain things in common. They have:

- a common purpose;
- some kind of structure;
- processes for co-ordinating activities;
- people carrying out distinct roles.

Having a common purpose does not of itself make an organisation. A mob can have a common purpose. It is building a structure and processes around a goal that creates an organisation.

In addition to the four common factors above, there is a need to define the organisation's purpose and objectives, to plan and co-ordinate the work, and to direct and control the activities of the people within the organisation. The fifth common factor is therefore management.

The following section summarises some of the major attempts at classifying organisations as defined above.

WAYS OF CLASSIFYING ORGANISATIONS

People have been trying to find ways of classifying organisations for many years, searching for a recognised method which will permit easy comparison across diverse areas of business and commerce. The main organisational classification theories are described below.

Weber

Weber[1] categorised organisations in terms of the types of authority exercised. He distinguished three types:

1. *The traditional organisation* – where authority is established by custom and long standing and unquestioned belief, for example the monarchy.
2. *The charismatic organisation* – where authority is derived from the outstanding personal qualities of the leader; modern examples might be Lonrho (Tiny Rowland) or Virgin (Richard Branson).
3. *The bureaucratic organisation* – where authority is based on the acceptance of formal rules and procedures, for example the Civil Service or the armed forces. Whereas the term 'bureaucracy' is now more often than not used in a pejorative sense, Weber used the term descriptively and highlighted the strengths of this kind of organisation.

This kind of analysis will not usually help greatly when comparing organisations as most will be bureaucracies in the above sense of the word.

Etzioni

Etzioni[2] analysed organisations in terms of power and involvement. Power is defined in terms of how it is exercised by the organisation and the individual's commitment to the organisation. Three types of power are identified:

1. *Coercive power* — relies on the use of threats or sanctions to enforce control, for example prisons.
2. *Remunerative power* — relies on the use of rewards and control of resources, for example commercial enterprises.
3. *Normative power* — relies on the general acceptance of the norms, values and beliefs of those exercising power, for example churches, charities, clubs.

Etzioni also defined three types of commitment:

1. *Alienative* — where the members are forced to accept involvement.
2. *Calculative* — where the members participate because of the rewards available to them.
3. *Moral* — where the members are committed to the goals and values of the organisation.

Etzioni considers that the key to analysing organisations on this basis is the concept of compliance. This is the product of the combination of power and involvement. A 'congruent' organisation is one in which power matches commitment. For example, where there is coercive power the involvement would be expected to be alienative; where there is remunerative power, calculative; and where there is normative power, moral. This is summarised in Figure 2.1.

While Etzioni's analysis might be useful in understanding the degree of commitment that may be shown by people in different situations it is not a particularly sophisticated way of comparing different organisations, because it has insufficient depth and too many organisations would not fit the model.

Types of power	Types of involvement		
	Alienative	Calculative	Moral
Coercive	X		
Remunerative		X	
Normative			X

X = congruent relationship

Figure 2.1   *The relationship between power and involvement in organisations*

Blau and Scott

Blau and Scott[3] classified organisations in terms of the main beneficiary. They identified four main groups of beneficiaries:

- The rank and file members;
- The owners or managers;
- The public who have contact with the organisation;
- The public in general.

These four groups are described as:

- mutual benefit;
- business;
- service;
- commonwealth.

This classification is useful in helping to understand organisations, as the prime beneficiaries will be the ones who determine the organisation's direction and strategy. It is particularly helpful when considering the role of organisations such as water companies. Who are the prime beneficiaries — the public at large or the shareholders? How can the need to provide a service to the public be balanced with the requirement to provide a return on investment? Should profits be reinvested or paid as dividends?

Burns and Stalker

Burns and Stalker[4] distinguished between what they describe as mechanistic and organismic management structures. The *mechanistic structure* is viewed as one which is more appropriate to stable conditions and is characterised by:

- clear differentiation between specialised tasks;
- precise definitions of tasks and the ways in which they should be carried out;
- a definite hierarchy for controlling work, decision making and communicating decisions;
- strong hierarchical relationships with an emphasis on loyalty and obedience;
- knowledge concentrated at the top of the hierarchy.

The *organismic structure* is more appropriate to changing conditions and is characterised by:

- specialised knowledge and experience which contribute to the organisation's overall objectives;

- jobs determined by the organisation's overall objectives;
- the constant redefinition of jobs;
- a network structure of control, authority and communication;
- commitment to the objectives of the organisation;
- stronger lateral communication and an emphasis on advice and information rather than instruction;
- knowledge spread throughout the organisation.

The reality is that there are probably few organisations that fit either model precisely. Most will contain both mechanistic and organismic elements. Furthermore, while the approach may cast some light on different organisation structures, it does not give a comprehensive means of clarifying organisations for comparison.

Katz and Kahn

Katz and Kahn[5] distinguished four broad types of organisation:

1. *Productive or economic organisations* — that are concerned with creation of wealth, manufacturing goods and providing services; these can be further subdivided according to industry sector.
2. *Maintenance organisations* — that are concerned with the socialisation of people to carry out other roles, such as schools.
3. *Adaptive organisations* — that create knowledge, develop and test theories and apply information to existing problems, for example universities and research bodies.
4. *Managerial or political organisations* — that are concerned with adjudication, co-ordination and control of resources, people and activities, for example the Government, political parties, trade unions.

Organisations can be further differentiated by:

- distinguishing between people and objects as the organisation's end results;
- distinguishing between the intrinsic rewards of the work, eg job satisfaction, and the extrinsic rewards, eg wages;
- distinguishing between the ease with which people can join or leave and the way the organisation is structured and rewards are allocated;
- reviewing the extent to which the organisation is in a 'steady state' with inputs equal to outputs, eg commercial enterprises will seek to maximise their return at the lowest cost.

Woodward

In a study of manufacturing firms Woodward[6] graded them according to ten levels of technical complexity, from simple small batch and unit production to the continuous flow production of liquids, gases and solids. Comparisons were then made with the numbers of levels of authority, spans of control of full-time supervisors, and the ratios of managers and supervisory staff to total personnel.

One of the most significant aspects of this study was that there appeared to be no clear link between the 'principles of organisation' and business success. The most successful companies were substantially different from each other.

Perrow

Perrow[7] extended the work relating to the impact of technology on organisations by considering:

- the extent to which tasks were predictable or unplanned;
- the extent to which the technology could be analysed and problems resolved through using routine procedures.

Lawrence and Lorsch

Lawrence and Lorsch[8] looked at organisations in terms of what they described as 'differentiation' and 'integration'. *Differentiation* was defined as the way in which managers viewed:

- the attainment of goals;
- their time orientation in terms of their planning horizons;
- interpersonal relationships, particularly in terms of management style;
- formality of organisation structure, particularly the extent to which it could be described as mechanistic or organismic.

Integration was defined as the degree of collaboration between departments with interdependent tasks.

It was generally found that different departments have different goals, different time horizons, environments and structures. While, for example, research might take a long-term view and have a structure and process that encouraged innovative thinking, the production role has to respond to the more immediate demands of meeting delivery dates and is, of necessity, more bureaucratically structured.

SUGGESTED BASIS FOR COMPARISON

The problem with adopting any one approach to classifying or analysing organisations is that it leaves out other key aspects. For example, concentrating just on the organisation's structure ignores the importance of the people within the organisation. The 'best' structure that can be devised will not increase efficiency and effectiveness if staff are poorly motivated. Advanced computer systems will not increase efficiency if staff are not trained in their use. Even well motivated staff will not give of their best if they are frustrated by the organisation's structure, systems or management. There are, therefore, a whole variety of factors to be taken into account when making comparisons or undertaking analysis.

It is also very difficult to lay down firm rules about what kinds of structure, processes and people an organisation needs to achieve success. There are those that break many of the 'rules' but still succeed, and there are those that have been held up as beacons of excellence but which have subsequently foundered, for example IBM. There is also the question of what constitutes organisational success. Survival is one measure, but how important are profitability, providing employment, social responsibility and so on? Many local authority direct services organisations, for example, face a dilemma — are they there to make a profit, provide a service or maintain a level of employment?

There may be just too many variables to make comprehensive analysis and comparison of organisations feasible. It is almost certainly the case that in organisations of any size and with varied functions, no one structure, management style or culture will be entirely appropriate for all functions. It is, however, still vital to make external comparisons to ensure that a company does not fall behind its competitors and that organisations generally make the best use of resources and provide the most economic, efficient and effective service possible.

The key factors that are of most value in making organisational comparisons are set out below, together with an explanation of their significance.

Industry

The kind of industry the organisation is in will have a fundamental effect on its structure, processes and people. The requirements of a hotel chain, an accountancy firm and a manufacturing company will be very different.

Size

Organisations will become more complex as they increase in size. They are likely to have a more formal structure and develop more rules and procedures to cope with the growth in complexity. Size can of course be measured in many ways and will vary substantially between industry sectors.

Technology

While the technology used will depend on the industry, being in the same industry does not guarantee identical processes. There are, for example, big differences between the car manufacturers Ford, Morgan and Volvo. However, the technology and processes used will affect the company's structure and the kind of people employed.

History and ownership

Whether the company is public or private sector or recently privatised, where the real control lies, political constraints and so on will all affect strategy, structure and internal processes.

Structure

Structure includes whether the company is organised on a geographical, functional or some other basis, spans of control, levels in the hierarchy, core operational and staff functions and so on. It will have a major impact on the way work is done and on the motivation and morale of employees.

Processes

Processes are those used for planning, controlling and organising work, for communicating vertically and laterally, for decision making, for employee management (eg the reward system, performance management) and so on. A significant use of information technology, for example, will have an impact on structure, people and the other processes of the organisation.

People

Factors concerning people include total numbers, the numbers in each business unit or division, numbers in each grade or salary band, different levels of qualifications and experience, the ratios of staff/administrative support roles to operational roles and so on.

Stage of development

For some companies the organisation's stage of development might be important. For example, is a particular organisation at the beginning of a growth phase when another is operating in a mature market?

Performance measures

In a sense performance measures are different from the other factors as they may be regarded as output measures, ie what the organisation produces, rather than input measures, ie the parameters and conditions affecting those outputs. However, measures such as profitability, return on capital, earnings per share, staff turnover and absenteeism levels, numbers of disputes and grievances and staff attitudes are important mechanisms for comparing the performance of organisations.

PRIVATE SECTOR AND PUBLIC SECTOR ORGANISATIONS

One main distinction when considering organisation types is that between the public and private sectors. Typically, public sector organisations are those such as local authorities which are publicly owned and which exist to provide services to the public, not solely for the profit or benefit of one particular group. Private sector organisations, on the other hand, exist primarily to achieve commercial objectives and to provide a good return to their shareholders. It is often argued, principally by those in the private sector, that the profit motive and competition lead to more efficient organisations, which otherwise would not survive in the marketplace.

The distinction between the public and private sectors is, however, becoming much more blurred. Many former public sector bodies have been privatised or commercialised and now have to make profits, for example, British Gas, British Telecom and the water companies. This trend shows no sign of abating and is general in Europe including, for example, Copenhagen Airport and, at the time of writing, it is to be extended in France to include companies such as Rhône Poulenc and Banque Nationale de Paris. It is being extended in the UK even to cover such areas as prisons. A more useful approach might therefore be to distinguish between profit-making and non-profit-making organisations.

Increasing privatisation does bring with it some fundamental questions about the extent to which a public service should, for example, concentrate on improving services rather than maximising the return to its investors. Are these services for the benefit of all consumers or just for their shareholders? Striking the balance is not easy.

CONCLUSION

As we have shown, there is no simple way of classifying organisations so that everyone will recognise a particular type more or less instantly. Useful theories and models have been developed over more than half a century but none is sufficiently comprehensive to capture the dynamics of organisations and therefore allow meaningful comparisons across industries and sectors.

That is not to say that some of the work does not have practical and useful applications. Woodward's analysis, for example, is still seen as a valuable empirical methodology for assessing organisations where technology and technical complexity are significant.

In conclusion, therefore, we would stress the need to be clear about the use to which organisational classification systems are to be put. If it is simply to distinguish between companies in the same sector with largely the same technology and culture, then a simple model of size, geography and processes will probably be sufficient to draw useful conclusions and even distinguish the good and better performers. If, on the other hand, the aim is a comparison across sectors and large numbers of organisations are involved, be cautious — results can be greatly affected by the choice of methodology.

References

[1] Weber, M (1964) *The Theory of Social and Economic Organisation*, translated by A M Henderson and T Parsons, Oxford University Press, Oxford.

[2] Etzioni, A (1975) *A Comparative Analysis of Complex Organisations*, Free Press, New York.

[3] Blau, P M and Scott, W R (1966) *Formal Organisations*, Routledge and Kegan Paul, London.

[4] Burns, T and Stalker, G M (1966) *The Management of Innovation*, Tavistock Publications, London.

[5] Katz, D and Kahn, R L (1978) *The Social Psychology of Organisations*, Wiley, New York.

[6] Woodward, J (1980) *Industrial Organisation — Theory and Practice*, Oxford University Press, Oxford.

[7] Perrow, C (1967) *Organisational Analysis: A Sociological View*, Tavistock, London.

[8] Lawrence, P R and Lorsch, J W (1969) *Organisation and Environment*, Irwin, New York.

Organisational Analysis

WHY ANALYSE?

There are many examples of companies that succeed despite apparently breaking the 'rules' about efficiency and effectiveness and the like, and conversely there are those that fail when they apparently should not. However, it would generally be agreed that it is important to measure how well the organisation is doing at any particular time. Not only is such information essential to managers, but it is likely to be demanded by shareholders, the public and the Government. Effective diagnosis of the current state of play in the organisation is also a prerequisite for any proposed changes. The purpose of this chapter is to examine ways in which organisational effectiveness can be measured once the overall direction and strategy have been established. The development of the organisation's mission and strategy is described in Chapter 4.

OVERALL APPROACH

In analysing any organisation there are three elements that need to be reviewed once a clear mission and strategy are in place:

1. *Organisation structure* — this describes how accountabilities, tasks and roles are allocated within the organisation. It is important because of the impact it can have on the way people perform their jobs and on the effectiveness of the organisation's processes.
2. *Processes* — these are the mechanisms by which the organisation's activities are carried out and they will usually

determine how the organisation is structured, although they may be tailored to suit the structure. They will also influence the kind of people employed.

3. *People* — the central resource of any organisation is its people. Raw material remains just that without their intervention. They in turn determine the organisation's structure and processes. How many times are the theoretically most logical structures and processes changed to suit individuals?

While each of these three elements will need to be examined separately in depth, no analysis would be complete unless it reviewed all three and took account of the interrelationship between them. They should all support the organisation's mission and strategy (see Figure 3.1).

CULTURE AND CLIMATE

The organisation's culture and climate will also have an impact on its efficiency and effectiveness and, therefore, analysing them is also an important part of gaining a full understanding of the organisation.

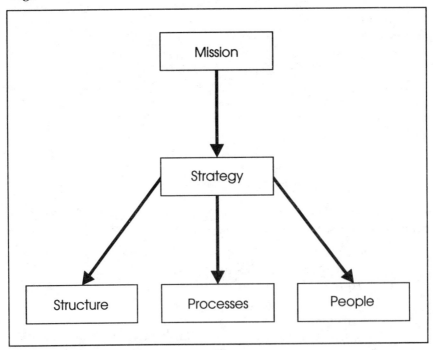

Figure 3.1   *Major elements of the organisation*

The organisation's culture is made up of the deeply held beliefs about the way the organisation should operate. It is the organisation's value system and will influence the way in which work is carried out and how employees behave. People who may be very able and efficient in their own right, but who nevertheless do not fit into the culture, for example because of the way they dress, will be unlikely to achieve long-term success in the organisation (see Figure 3.2).

Reinforcing the culture

The pressure to conform to a particular culture is very strong. This is demonstrated by many of the City of London's financial sector companies, although they are by no means unique. In one particular company the secret of success was described as 'getting yourself a Burberry raincoat', and woe betide anyone who had the temerity to wear a brown suit! As exaggerated and jocular as these comments and reactions might appear, they did actually help to enforce a fairly rigid but unwritten dress code, which in turn supported the wider culture.

One of the problems with the kind of culture that seeks a high degree of conformity is that people become unwilling to question the official view, even though they may feel it to be wrong.

The climate is the prevalent atmosphere in the organisation, encompassing the feelings and emotions of the people within it. It is their perception of what it is like to work there. As the employees' feelings and attitudes will clearly have an impact on the way they carry out their work, they are an important part of analysing the organisation (see Figure 3.3).

BUSINESS ANALYSIS

This business analysis section covers a number of different approaches to analysing the organisation in its entirety, not just the individual elements of structure, processes and people. The term 'business' in this context also covers the public sector.

Swot Analysis

'SWOT' stands for Strengths, Weaknesses, Opportunities and Threats.

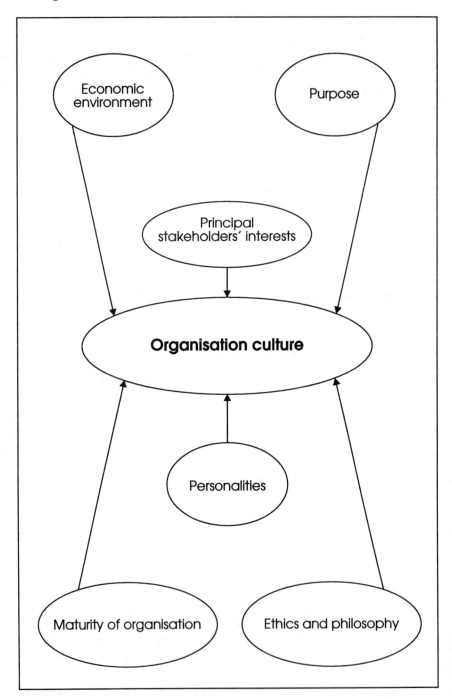

Figure 3.2   *Factors affecting organisation culture*

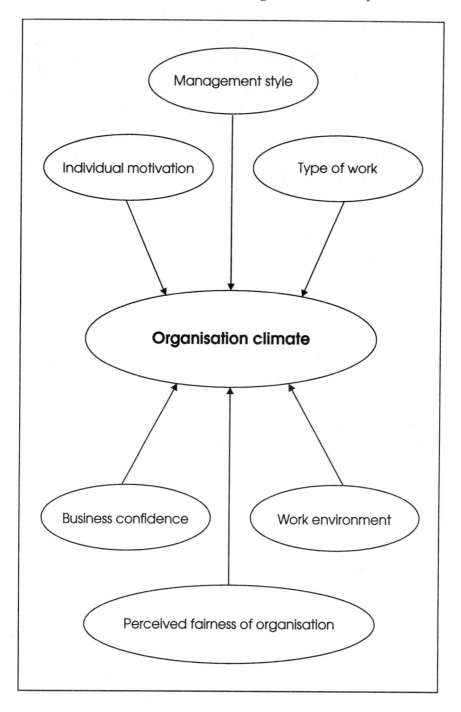

Figure 3.3 *Factors affecting organisational climate*

Strengths may be described as those positive aspects of the organisation which may lead to further opportunities and which can therefore be built on. What are the company's competitive advantages and unique selling points?

Weaknesses are any deficiencies in the company's skills and resources. Consideration needs to be given as to how these can be remedied, for example by acquisition, merger or training and development.

Opportunities describe those events in the external environment that the organisation may be able to take advantage of. These are likely to arise from changes in technology, markets, products, legislation and so on.

Threats are dangers or problems that might damage the position of the organisation, for example the introduction of a new product by a competitor, changes to safety standards, changing fashions, or problems with suppliers or customers.

Whereas strengths and weaknesses primarily concern the internal workings of the organisation, opportunities and threats arise primarily from the external environment.

Value for money

Value for money (VFM) reviews of public sector services are typically undertaken by accountancy firms as an extension of their auditing role.

While the term 'value for money' is now in common usage, it is generally accepted that the definition includes the three elements of economy, efficiency and effectiveness. These terms are defined by Butt and Palmer as:[1]

Economy — the practice by management of the virtues of thrift and good housekeeping leading to resources in appropriate quality and quantity at the lowest cost.

Efficiency — making sure the maximum useful output is gained from the resources devoted to each activity, or, alternatively, that only the minimum level of resources are devoted to achieving a given level of output.

Effectiveness — ensuring that the output from any given activity level (or the impact that services have on a community) is achieving the desired results.

To put it another way, the organisation needs to ensure that not only is it doing things right but that it is also doing the right things.

Typically, VFM reviews might cover some or all of the following aspects of the organisation:

- overall strategy and objectives, including the monitoring and review process;
- the performance measures and standards used by the organisation to assess economy and efficiency;
- the budgetary and financial control procedures in use;
- organisation structure and staffing levels;
- activity levels;
- overhead costs;
- detailed review of procedures and activities.

Of particular importance is the development of comprehensive performance measures which can be related to the level of service provision, for example the number of planning applications processed by the local authority, as well as the costs.

Improving value for money — Case study

A typical example of a VFM exercise was one carried out in a London borough to review the central administration service in terms of its economy, efficiency and effectiveness.

This entailed looking at the processes, numbers and levels of staff employed, output measures (numbers of invoices processed, numbers of keystrokes for data input etc) and structure of the central services. While a number of improvements were suggested to working methods and there was some evidence of over-resourcing, one of the most significant findings concerned the computer system used in one department. Despite having a comprehensive data processing system, staff were still using a card index system to maintain the same information. The card index data was used to check the accuracy of the computer data. Rather than saving work the system had created more.

The reason for this duplication was a lack of training and a consequent lack of confidence in the computer system. In fact the number of records and the amount of information required were so limited that a card index system was adequate for the organisation's needs.

Financial analysis

An important aspect of reviewing any organisation is analysing its financial stability. This is, of course, particularly relevant to commercial enterprises as their very existence is dependent on long-term financial strength. Such analysis is usually carried out by reviewing financial ratios and rates of return.

Financial ratios help to measure the company's profitability, liquidity and capital structure. However, they are of little value in isolation and should mainly be used only in comparison with industry norms. It is important to note that what may be a poor return on investment in one industry may be very good in another.

A note of caution that needs to be sounded about comparing two companies' accounts is that you cannot always be sure that you are comparing like with like, as different accounting conventions may be used by different companies. Accounts nevertheless remain one of the more objective sources of information.

Statistical analysis

There are many statistical analyses that can be undertaken to diagnose organisational health. Many of these will relate to productivity, for example numbers of invoices processed by clerical staff, the number of items produced by any particular work group as compared with others, or comparative staffing levels. However, there are also a number of less obvious measures that can be used to determine how well the organisation is performing. These include the following:

1. *Staff turnover* — this is usually expressed as a percentage. It will vary between industries and will be affected by the current state of the economy. In a recession, when jobs are more difficult to find, the turnover rate would be expected to be relatively low.

2. *Absenteeism and lateness* — absenteeism occurs when an employee who is scheduled for work at a particular time does not turn up. The national average annual number of days of absence in the UK is about nine per person, which compares very unfavourably with the rest of Europe (assuming that statistics are compiled with equal vigour and accuracy). Thus anything significantly higher than this figure should give cause for concern. Comparisons should be made between different work groups and job types to highlight any particular problem areas.

3. *Grievances and disputes* — it is perhaps self-evident that where a high number of disputes and grievances are raised by employees, there is likely to be low morale, with specific grievances perhaps being symptoms of a more deep-seated problem. It is as well to remember that only the tip of what has been described as the organisational iceberg is actually seen and there is a vast array of attitudes, fears and beliefs hidden beneath the surface.

4. *Employee attitudes* — as indicated above, although there are very often outward and obvious signs of dissatisfaction, this is

not always the case. It is valuable to seek the views of employees about the organisation, as it is important for them to be committed to its objectives if they are going to work effectively. This is considered further in Chapter 8. However, an important point to remember about attitude surveys is that once they have been conducted, feedback on the results should be given to employees and action taken where appropriate. If this is not done the technique is liable to be discredited and confidence in management undermined.

Some of the more valuable attitude surveys are those that seek to measure employees' perceptions of organisational climate and leadership style. Their results will help managers determine whether or not messages about the organisation's overall mission and objectives have been understood and acted on. They will also be strong indicators of any actual or potential organisational problems.

ORGANISATION STRUCTURE ANALYSIS

There are a number of techniques that may be used to analyse the structure of organisations. Their fundamental aims should be to determine whether:

- the existing structure is appropriate to the needs of the organisation;
- it supports the mission and strategy;
- it provides the most logical and cost-effective grouping of functions;
- it is a structure that gets the best out of the people in the organisation.

Some of the main techniques for assessing these factors are set out below.

Organisation design criteria

An organisation design criterion is a basic principle or characteristic of an organisation which will help it to achieve its strategic objectives and meet its critical success factors (see Chapter 4).

To analyse a structure on this basis it is necessary to:

- determine which criteria are of central importance to the organisation — for example, the desire to provide a strong, locally based customer support service might suggest a geographically based structure, whereas a need for an effective corporate approach and tight cost control might suggest a more centralised structure;

- measure their impact on the previously identified critical success factors (see Chapter 4);
- weight these criteria both in terms of their current importance to the organisation and also in terms of the impact they would be likely to have on organisation strategy;
- rank these criteria and test them against different organisational types — examples of organisation design criteria are given below, and a completed rating worksheet (as used by Hay Management Consultants) is shown in Figure 3.4.

Examples of organisation design criteria for an international company

1. Integrates all activities across the group to ensure conformity to corporate strategy.
2. Provides for rapid and effective decision making at the point closest to the customer.
3. Provides effective communications within the company.
4. Focuses attention on results.
5. Secures effective employee relations.
6. Encourages the development of highly skilled managers.
7. Provides a swift response to market opportunities on a global basis.

To complete the worksheet:

1. List the criteria.
2. Rate criteria as currently perceived.
3. Estimate the impact on strategy.
4. Rate the impact on previously identified critical success factors (CSFs).
5. Calculate current rating + strategic impact + number of times it relates to a CSF.
6. Rank the criteria based on the total scores.

The overall issue to be considered in reviewing the organisation design criteria is what the organisation structure is to achieve. Once it is known what direction to take, it is much easier to decide on the appropriate route.

Organisation design criteria	Current rating	Strategic impact	CSF1	CSF2	CSF3	CSF4	CSF5	CSF6	CSF7	CSF8	Count	Total score
								Critical success factor impact				
1. Integration	1	2	X			X					2	4
2. Decision making	2	3		X		X	X	X			4	9
3. Communication	4	1	X			X			X	X	4	9
4. Results focused	3	2		X	X		X				3	8
5. Employee relations	4	2	X							X	2	8
6. Management	3	1		X							1	5
7. Responsiveness	5	3	X		X			X		X	4	12

Current rating: A = Excellent (1)
B = Good (2)
C = Fair (3)
D = Poor (4)
E = Embryonic (5)

Strategic impact: H = High (3)
M = Medium (2)
L = Low (1)

Figure 3.4 *Ranking organisation design criteria – worksheet (Hay)*

Job analysis

Although job analysis is covered in detail in Chapter 6, it is mentioned here as an important part of organisational review. In particular, jobs should be reviewed to determine any overlaps in tasks and accountabilities, both vertically with subordinates or superordinates and horizontally with colleagues across the organisation structure.

One way of detecting such overlaps is through an inter-accountability matrix. In the Hay Management Consultants' approach, the major functions of the organisation, or more probably a particular part of it, are listed and plotted against the posts that have accountability for the delivery of these services, or for supporting their delivery. Such an analysis should indicate which post has the prime accountability, where that accountability may be shared by a number of people and where a particular post is in a support role. Not only will such an analysis show overlaps, but it will also indicate where there are gaps with no one person being held accountable for a particular work area. An example of an inter-accountability matrix is shown in Figure 3.5.

Accountability	Post			
	Finance Director	Operations Director	HR Director	Sales Director
1 Develop business plan	S	S	S	S
2 Develop reward strategy	C	C	P	C
3 Achieve operating targets	C	S	C	S
4 Develop new markets	C	C	C	P

P = prime accountability for results

S = shared accountability for results

C = contributes to results but not directly accountable

Figure 3.5 *An inter-accountability matrix (Hay)*

To be effective, an analysis of the kind described must:

- be supported by accurate and agreed job descriptions;
- have regard to previously identified strategic objectives and action steps;
- be analysed by teams which include those holding the key posts covering the accountabilities described, otherwise incorrect assumptions might be made about where a particular accountability lies.

It should be noted that this kind of analysis can be extended beyond individual jobs to include particular organisational units and various kinds of activities carried out so that, in the final analysis, there is no misunderstanding about who is accountable for what.

The Wardale criteria

When considering vertically overlapping jobs, it may be useful to bear in mind the three criteria developed from the Wardale Report on top UK Civil Servants.[2] These are that there should be:

- a clear difference in the weight of jobs done at different levels;
- a different substance in purpose of the jobs at different levels, or to put it another way, the jobs at different levels should add some value to the overall organisation;
- a demonstrable requirement in the content of the job to integrate the work of the levels below and co-ordinate it with other areas of activity.

Where there are jobs which do not conform to the above criteria, then the number of levels should be examined with a view to reduction.

Spans of control

As indicated in Chapter 5 where the subject is considered in more detail, there is no magic formula for the ideal number of subordinates reporting to a boss. However, an examination of spans of control in conjunction with the number of levels in the organisation is a valuable analytical tool.

To undertake this analysis it is necessary to have job descriptions and organisation charts. The organisation chart will indicate at least the theoretical number of direct reports (often the reality is different) and the job descriptions will help to determine the precise roles being carried out.

It is probably healthy to be sceptical about structures which have one over one or one over two at a number of levels, or similar variants, but there are circumstances in which such structures can be justified, particularly in research or professional office environments. In general, the simpler and more uniform the job being supervised the larger the span of control, so the supervisor of a production line may have 20 to 30 direct reports, whereas greater complexity and variety necessitate fewer direct reports if co-ordination is to be effective.

PROCESS ANALYSIS

While a review of organisation structure is an essential component of improving the effectiveness of an organisation, it is also vital to examine the processes by which activities are carried out and managed. Many of these will cut across functional or departmental boundaries and it is important, therefore, to ensure that there is effective management horizontally within the organisation. This may often be seen, for example, in the shape of project teams composed of people from a range of disciplines brought together to achieve one specific objective or programme. However, a classic organisation problem occurs when different functions such as sales, marketing, production, and research and development all have completely different priorities, resulting in internal conflict and a less effective service to the customer. Processes should be designed to ensure that they support corporate objectives and provide the required quality and types of products and services.

Approaches for analysing the organisation's processes are considered below.

Business process re-engineering

This relatively new approach, which is also called business process improvement or value chain analysis, reviews the overall horizontal workflows and processes in the organisation, not just to improve then but to fundamentally re-examine them.

The approach:

● examines the processes that are critical to the success of the organisation;
● determines those processes which are priorities in terms of giving the company competitive advantage;
● determines the types of change or new investment required to ensure the maximum efficiency and effectiveness of these processes;

- determines what changes to aspects of the company's strategy and structure may be necessary;
- reviews managerial accountabilities and redefines jobs as required to ensure that the processes can be optimised where possible.

The essential difference between business process re-engineering and other techniques is essentially one of focus. Processes actually in place are examined but from a multi-disciplinary viewpoint. It is not just a question of improving efficiency but also of re-appraising strategy and structure. The starting point for this type of review should be the customers or clients, with systems being developed to support their needs and requirements.

Systems analysis

While systems analysis is really the province of the data processing specialist, some of the tools in use, such as data flow diagrams, are very useful for mapping workflows. By following a structured systems analysis and design methodology it is possible to gain detailed information about existing systems, including where work comes from and goes to and the detailed requirements of the users of those systems. Even for the non-DP specialist such an approach is useful for micro-level design of the organisation's processes.

Activity profiling

Activity profiling is a methodology developed by Price Waterhouse Urwick to analyse the relative contribution made by different activities to the achievement of organisational objectives. In this analysis essential activities and the costs of those activities, including manpower costs, resource usage, opportunity costs and so on, as well as any cash outlay, are compared and ratios produced. From this information it is possible to compare the cost of the activity with the contribution that activity makes towards the achievement of core objectives. Clearly there will be some activities which are fundamental to the organisation and essential, whereas others may be discretionary. Information can be gathered about these two types of activity and the relative contribution measured against the cost. Decisions can then be made about how resources could be allocated in the future (see Figure 3.6 on page 43).

Zero-based budgeting

There has always been a tendency in large organisations to base the figures for the current year's budgets on what was spent in the previous year, with an allowance for inflation. The zero-based budgeting (ZBB) approach requires that every activity with a separate budget head must first of all justify its existence, and then indicate what level of spending is required to meet likely needs.

ZBB works on a 'bottom-up' basis with individual budget holders having to justify their budget projections and with each activity being ranked according to priority. The budget projections are then reviewed at different levels in the organisation. Finally, top level decisions may be made about priorities and service provision.

While this is designed as a process to be used on an ongoing basis in an organisation, it is clear that it entails a significant amount of time in discussion and implementation and can also be viewed as threatening. However, it is valuable as an analytical tool since it does force the organisation to question its assumptions.

Similar considerations apply to the approach known as the programme planning and budgeting system (PPBS) which establishes priorities on a 'top-down' basis and therefore encourages a corporate approach to the establishment of budgets.

Work measurement

The techniques of work measurement are well established, particularly in the case of work study methodology for manual and craft jobs. In such jobs, and also for routine clerical tasks, it is possible to measure relatively accurately the time taken to produce certain levels of output. It is, therefore, straightforward to assess current productivity through observation or by asking individuals to maintain records of the activities they undertake. While there are many well established standards, for example the number of keystrokes that an average performer can carry out in a day, typing speeds or production quotas, this kind of measurement becomes more difficult for non-routine aspects of work, such as fault finding.

There are also a large number of jobs for which the techniques of work measurement are inappropriate. These include, for example, jobs where it is the quality of thinking rather than any tangible output that is the important consideration. This would apply to most professional and managerial jobs, where the measures have to be based more on customer satisfaction and competences.

Communication processes

There would probably be little disagreement that effective communication is vital to organisational success and there is, therefore, a strong case for trying to measure the processes of communication. Although the organisation chart will show the formal lines of communication, there are of course many informal links and these may be the more important sources of information. Everyone knows about the power of the grapevine.

Measuring communication in an organisation can be achieved using sociograms (see Figure 3.7) which map the number of interactions occurring between different members of a particular work group. In this way those who are central communication links, and those who are peripheral, can easily be identified. This in turn has implications for the organisation's structure and the roles carried out by certain posts. A number of proprietary tools have been developed to measure these communication flows.

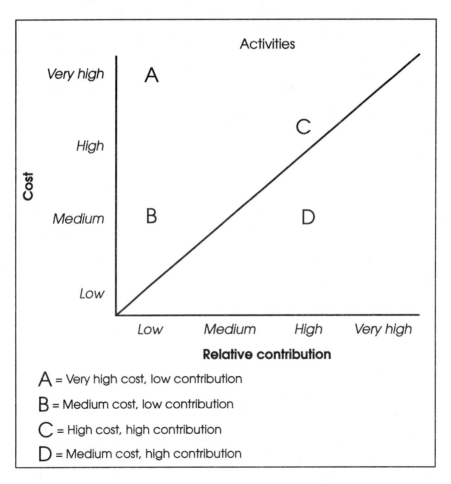

Figure 3.6 *Activity profiling*

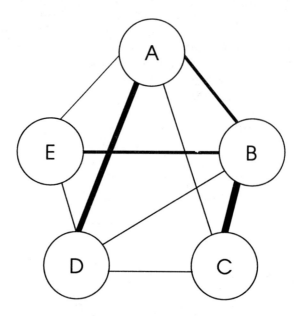

Thickness of line = volume of interactions

Figure 3.7   *A sociogram*

PEOPLE ANALYSIS

While reviews of organisations frequently concentrate on structure and processes, it is vital to review the organisation's human resources as they will make the structure and processes work. Effective and well motivated employees will overcome the deficiencies of poor structure and processes, while the best structure and processes will not work without employees' full co-operation.

Psychometric tests and assessment centres

Two broad approaches which are increasingly being used are psychometric tests and assessment centres.

Psychometric tests are structured questionnaires, presented in written form, or computer generated. They are aimed usually at assessing measures of ability, such as numerical reasoning, or capacities, such as building and developing relationships.

Whereas tests are typically wholly objective and produce fairly hard numerical outputs, assessment centres are based on observation of performance. A number of tasks are undertaken either individually or in groups and observed by assessors who then classify the behaviour in relation to its strength on a range of dimensions of skill or competence.

Assessment centres are particularly powerful in determining fit to future roles that may not have been experienced before. The exercises undertaken are simulations of such roles but do not require specific knowledge of them. For instance, an analytical planning exercise might be given to assess the person's capability for dealing practically with numbers and making sound business judgements, but particular knowledge of the industry concerned will not be required.

Assessment centres can also be classed as 'development centres'. In these the emphasis is not so much on identifying suitability for a particular job but areas for further growth and development.

Both psychometric instruments and assessment centre technology require specialised development and use. Training in interpretation of psychometrics is important because such interpretation does not end once the 'numbers' have been produced. It is usual to relate any particular set of results to a table of norms, ie the performance of an appropriate group, and some skill is required to decide the right group for comparison. Skill is also, of course, required in the first place to decide the appropriate range of tests for a person to take.

Psychometric instruments in particular have sometimes been blamed for being 'unfair' or 'biased'. The wrong tests, or tests wrongly applied, can be misleading, but the same will apply to any other source of information about people. Careful thought must be applied to the choice of tests. The range and variety are very wide — at least 2000 psychometric tests of different sorts are currently in print in the English language alone.

Right sizing

Right sizing is a methodology developed by Hay Management Consultants, based on a zero-based budgeting approach and designed to determine the appropriate levels of resources for particular levels of service. It is designed to help the organisation change the level of the resources allocated to a particular activity, either upwards or downwards, to meet the requirements of markets, competition, or economic and other constraints.

The approach consists of the following stages:

1. *Planning* in order to agree the scope and framework of the

exercise, including identifying areas where there is a real potential for savings and the priority outcomes to be achieved. It should be stressed that the approach is not focused just on savings, because it may well be that there are areas in which service provision has to be increased. It is at the planning stage that the organisation's priorities in this respect will need to be established.

2. *Activity analysis*, which entails gaining a detailed understanding of how the resources are currently used in the organisation. This involves analysing and evaluating activities carried out within distinct functions and cost centres.

3. *Identification of alternative levels of service*, which entails identifying the various options open to the organisation and their associated costs. For example, it may be possible to provide a slightly enhanced service which will have both benefits and costs. These would both be recorded. They could also be compared with the costs and benefits of providing a slightly diminished level of service. These different levels of service can be compared using a range of performance indicators which includes cost, quality and service to the customer.

4. *Determination of the resource implications* of providing each level of service. What, for example, would be the manpower implications of providing management information more frequently and in more detail?

5. *Development of a rating scale* to provide a basis for rating and prioritising competing claims for resources. The key issue here is the impact of these resources on the strategic priorities of the organisation.

6. *Ranking of levels of service*. A panel of senior managers reviews each level of service to determine the appropriate rankings.

7. *Production of a priority listing* of levels of activity ranked in terms of their impact on the organisation's strategic priorities. Against this ranking the incremental and cumulative costs for each level of activity can be shown.

8. *Deciding the overall level of resource allocation* and the point beyond which service levels and objectives will not be funded.

The final outcome of an exercise of this kind should be cost reductions, a more logical allocation of resources, and a better focus of those resources on strategic priorities.

Attitude surveys

The use of employee attitude surveys has been mentioned earlier. They can be of considerable value, particularly to determine how the informal structure of the organisation works, to ascertain the climate and culture of the organisation and to gain views about the prevalent management style (which is part of the organisation culture).

Identifying the different types of organisation culture can assist in understanding the organisation and is particularly valuable when used to compare individual attitudes to it. Where there is a mismatch between the organisation's culture and the individual's preferred culture, problems will be likely to result. One of the more useful ways of classifying organisation culture is that proposed by Harrison[3] who describes the different types as follows:

1. *Power culture* — in which there is a central power source which exercises strong control over the organisation. It is characterised by few rules and procedures, little bureaucracy and by decisions being achieved more by influence than on purely logical grounds.
2. *Role culture* — in which there are formal roles and procedures, with work being allocated logically according to the tasks to be undertaken. In this culture the position becomes more important than the personality of the individual.
3. *Task culture* — in which most of the emphasis is on getting the job done and the organisation is therefore structured to bring together the appropriate resources and people to achieve results. The matrix organisation is a typical example of this kind of culture, which encourages team working.
4. *Person culture* — which exists mainly to serve the people within it. Examples are partnerships, social groups and some small consulting firms.

Analysing the culture of the organisation is important for determining whether it is appropriate to the circumstances and whether the people within the organisation subscribe to it.

CONCLUSION

There are many different ways of analysing organisations. The various approaches, used with discretion, are valuable for assessing organisational effectiveness and for determining where improvements can be made. They are, therefore, important elements in the design of organisations for achieving high motivation and morale among employees.

References

1   Butt, H A and Palmer, D R (1985) *Value for Money in the Public Sector —
     The Decision Maker's Guide*, Blackwell, Oxford.
2   Civil Service Department (1981) 'A Chain of Command Review'
     (unpublished).
3   Harrison, R (1972) 'How to describe your organization', *Harvard
     Business Review*, Sept–Oct.

Mission and Strategy

THE CONCEPT OF MISSION

The mission of an organisation may be described as a general statement which defines the organisation's essential or fundamental purpose or philosophy. It is a statement which answers the question, 'Why does this organisation exist?'

Probably the main advantage of a mission statement is that it helps to give employees a clear sense of what the organisation is all about. This, in turn, is likely to increase their clarity about their own objectives and increase their commitment to achieving them. As Peter Drucker[1] has stated:

A business is not defined by its name, statutes, or articles of incorporation. It is defined by the business mission. Only a clear definition of the mission and purpose of the organisation makes possible clear and realistic business objectives.

Research by the Ashridge Strategic Management Centre[2] has indicated that in developing a mission the following guiding principles should be followed:

1. The mission should ideally be developed over a period of time, being more likely to take years than months.
2. There has to be consensus among the top team.
3. The actions of the managers will more effectively communicate their belief in the organisation's values than will words.
4. It is essential for the top team to visibly support the mission.
5. There needs to be continuity in the top team to achieve the necessary consensus and to enable them to develop their ideas and attain consistency.
6. Mission statements should make an impact and reflect the personality of the organisation and its leadership.

7. Strategy and values should be formulated together.
8. Managers should make clear the link between behaviours and values.

This research also showed that the development of a mission would be inappropriate where the organisation's strategy was changing, where the top team was unlikely to remain stable or where there were strong differences between team members.

WHAT SHOULD BE INCLUDED IN A MISSION STATEMENT

Most mission statements include many of the following elements:

*   *customers or clients* — a statement about the organisation's customer or client base;
*   *products or services* — a description of the organisation's main products or services;
*   *technology* — a description of the organisation's main technology;
*   *markets* — the principal market or markets in which the organisation operates;
*   *employees* — the organisation's attitudes and beliefs about its employees;
*   *society* — the organisation's stance within and contribution to the wider society of which it is part;
*   *public image* — how the organisation would like to be perceived by the public at large;
*   *basic philosophy* — the organisation's fundamental values and beliefs, including how its members view it;
*   *boundaries* — the boundaries, whether geographical or other, within which the organisation operates;
*   *economic objectives* — the fundamental economic goals of the organisation, which are more likely to be expressed in terms of long-term growth and survival than short-term profitability.

FEATURES OF MISSION STATEMENTS

To be effective, a mission statement should have the following characteristics:

1. It should state the fundamental *purpose* of the organisation in a way that will inspire those within it.
2. It should communicate a *vision* of what the organisation wants to be like.

3. *Boundaries* should be clearly stated so that there is a clear focus for the organisation.
4. The *meaning* of the statement should be clear to everyone.
5. The statement should provide *guidance* in drawing up strategic and operating decisions.
6. The statement should contain an indication of the organisation's *values* sufficient to guide people's behaviour.
7. The statement should reflect the *character* of the organisation and be presented in a way that has an impact and captures the imagination.

PREPARING A MISSION STATEMENT

The first step in drawing up a mission statement is to decide whether or not such a statement is needed and whether it will be supported. Assuming that the value of a mission statement has been established, the following steps will be necessary to ensure its effective introduction and to provide the guiding light for future action.

An outline statement should be prepared, probably by the chief executive, outlining his or her basic perception of the organisation's purpose in accordance with the criteria outlined above, and this should then be discussed at the appropriate management team meeting. The aim at this meeting should be to gain top management commitment to the philosophy and purpose outlined and to mould the statement into something that those senior managers can identify with and give wholehearted support to.

While this top management commitment is essential, there is a danger of the discussions resulting in a statement which is either a weak compromise which fails to give the required strength and clarity of direction, or which is too convoluted to have a strong impact or convey the essential character of the organisation.

The basic statement should be capable of being crystallised into a single sentence which is readily understandable and has an immediate impact.

The next stage is to expand the mission statement into its various components or goals. These will take into account the areas which the organisation sees as fundamental to its overall purpose and are likely to include many of the headings listed in the above discussion of what a mission statement should contain.

In drawing up the components of the mission statement, the organisation will need to take account of the expectations of the managers and employees, shareholders, consumers, and other outside bodies such as Government departments. Some assumptions will also have to be made about the future in terms of political, economic and social trends and also those that are likely to affect the particular industry or product area in which the company is operating. The organisation will need to bear in mind both the external factors affecting its operations and the internal ones such as the quality of its human resources, systems and organisation structure and technological developments.

Finally, the mission and the philosophy behind it should be communicated to the organisation's employees and, where appropriate, customers. The mission should not be communicated simply by sending out a memo, but should be presented and seen to be actively supported by members of senior management.

PITFALLS TO BE AVOIDED

There are a number of dangers to be avoided when drafting a mission statement:

- The statement should not be too general or vague, otherwise it will be inadequate to help guide the organisation's strategy.
- Conversely, the statement should not be too specific — it should not need changing every year.
- The organisation needs to be careful not to produce a 'wish list' or 'motherhood' statement.
- The statement should not be so diluted by careful terminology that the character and impact of the message are lost.
- It is unlikely that the mission statement can be developed at one shot and it will probably need to be refined over many months, providing that the essential impact is not lost.
- The statement must not be driven by the narrow sectional interests of one particular group but must be universally acceptable throughout the organisation.
- The statement should not be a list of performance measures — these come later.
- While the mission may be an ideal, it must be an achievable one, otherwise it will quickly fall into disrepute and be ignored.
- Finally, the mission has to have the support of the managers and employees in the organisation, or it will founder.

EXAMPLES OF MISSION STATEMENTS

Wellcome

Wellcome is an international pharmaceutical company dedicated to the discovery and marketing of products that promote human health and the quality of life. We aim to achieve superior growth in market share, earnings per share and shareholder value to the benefit of customers, employees, shareholders and the community at large.

Kingfisher

It is our intention to have quality businesses, capable of maintaining leadership positions in long-term growth markets; capable of offering everyday low prices and superior value to the customer and of operating at simultaneously high levels of productivity and investment in people, customer service and the community at large.

Cadbury Schweppes

Our task is to build on our traditions of quality and value, to provide brands, products, financial results and management performance that meet the interests of our shareholders, consumers, employees, customers, suppliers and the communities in which we operate.

Enterprise Oil

Enterprise Oil is one of the world's leading independent oil exploration and production companies. Our objective is to provide shareholders with capital and income growth through the discovery, acquisition and development of oil and gas reserves. In all of our activities we are committed to promoting the health and safety of staff and contractors and protecting the environment.

ORGANISATIONAL GOALS

Many books on organisation theory refer to the concept of organisational goals. An organisation's goals can be seen as the fundamental purposes and values of that organisation and are likely to be expressed in terms of future expectations. In this sense, they are really the mission statement broken down into its various components.

Whether or not these aspects of the organisation's mission are described as goals, such statements are important because they:

- give a focus and direction to the whole of the organisation;
- help to ensure the commitment of the organisation's employees in working towards a common purpose;
- help to ensure clarity of overall direction;
- help to determine the detailed strategy and objectives;
- set performance standards for the organisation against which organisational achievements can be measured.

In overall terms, the mission and goals of the organisation will determine the kind of strategy and structure it will have and the kinds of processes, products and people required.

EXAMPLES OF ORGANISATIONAL GOALS

Tesco

Tesco is committed to:

- offering customers the best value for money and the most competitive prices of any national superstore chain;
- meeting the needs of customers by constantly seeking and acting on their opinions regarding product quality, choice, innovation, store facilities and service;
- providing shareholders with outstanding returns on their investment;
- improving profitability through investment in efficient stores and distribution depots, in productivity improvements and in new technology;
- developing talents of its people through sound management and training practices, while rewarding them fairly with equal opportunities for all;
- working closely with suppliers to build long-term business relationships based on strict quality and price criteria;
- participating in the formulation of national food industry policies on key issues such as health, nutrition, hygiene, safety and animal welfare;
- supporting the well-being of the community and the protection of the environment.

RTZ

RTZ aims to act responsibly as a steward of the essential resources in its care so that they benefit both the countries in which they are found and the world at large which depends on them. At the same time RTZ seeks to create long-term wealth for its shareholders. It believes that these two objectives go hand in hand and that the one cannot be achieved without the other.

The policies underlying RTZ's strategy are:

- predominant focus on large scale, high quality mining opportunities which are capable of producing at low cost;
- willingness to invest continuously in on-going operations;
- geographical spread which provides some protection against single currency exposure and against regional political instability;
- product diversity which mitigates the pressures that can result from being dependent on too small a range of commodities;
- attention to the quality of projects, rather than attempting to select fashionable commodities;
- operating practices which are geared to maximising long-term economic value, not short-term reported earnings;
- selection and promotion of high calibre management committed to improve the quality of the operations continuously;
- delegation of considerable authority to operating management leaving the centre to concentrate on strategic direction and act as the catalyst for the cross-fertilisation of best practice in all aspects of the business.

FORMAL AND INFORMAL GOALS

An organisation's mission and goals do not have an independent life of their own, but are products of the people of the organisation. Those who are drawing up the organisation's mission and goals will usually be the management board and the senior executives. However, in carrying out this exercise they will need to be aware of the constraints on them in terms of both the internal and the external environment. If the organisation's goals do not take account of, for example, Government policy, the economic situation, the organisation's capabilities or the attitudes of the employees, then the result may be a 'wish list' which is unattainable. Such a list would quickly fall into disrepute and would be of no practical value.

It is essential, therefore, that the stated formal goals of the organisation are practical and take account of what is achievable.

The people within the organisation will have their own particular goals, and it is generally agreed by writers on management that the most effective way of motivating people is to ensure that they can achieve their own goals by achieving those of the organisation. If individual goals are tending to pull in a different direction, overall performance and effectiveness will be undermined.

STRATEGY AND OBJECTIVES

Objectives state more specifically how the mission and goals of the organisation are to be achieved. They identify specific aims for the organisation.

Drucker states that:

> Objectives are needed in every area where performance and results directly and vitally affect the survival and prosperity of the business.

He identifies eight key areas:

1. *Market standing* — which market the company wants to be in and the desired market share.
2. *Innovation* — development of new products or services to meet marketing objectives or because of obsolescence, improvements in production processes and so on.
3. *Productivity* — ensuring the optimum utilisation of resources and the value added by the production process.
4. *Physical and financial resources* — the plant, machines, offices and finance required to ensure attainment of the organisation's goals.
5. *Profitability* — return on capital, net sales and so on.
6. *Manager performance and development* — goal setting, job design and management development.
7. *Worker performance and attitude* — in terms of employer relations.
8. *Public responsibility* — in terms of the social and political responsibilities of the organisation.

Objectives should have the following features:

- each objective should describe a separate and distinct contribution to the organisation's mission, rather than being a combination of a number of different contributions;
- objectives should focus on the end result to be achieved rather than the means of achieving it;

- each objective should emphasise the action that leads to the end result, but not the detailed activities that are necessary to achieve that result;
- objectives should be explicit about the nature and direction of the change required but without any specific timescale or output target.

Usually it is unlikely that the company will need to set out more than eight main organisational objectives. The headings suggested by Drucker should be sufficient to cover the main areas in which objectives need to be set, although they could be described in different ways. For example, the importance rightly attached by most organisations to quality is such that this is likely to be a main objective in itself.

DEVELOPING A STRATEGY

The strategic planning process is a structured way of clarifying organisational objectives, determining how those objectives will be achieved, and checking progress towards their attainment for the organisation as a whole. The strategic planning horizon will usually be several years and should include an analysis of the organisation as well as of the external environment. Similarly the process should identify those factors that are critical to the success of the organisation and also opportunities for synergy, which are discussed further below. The overall process is summarised in Figure 4.1.

Determining strategy

Following the formulation of its strategic objectives, the organisation should carry out what is generally described as a SWOT analysis. As described above (page 29), this is an analysis of the organisation's strengths and weaknesses and the threats and opportunities in the external environment. Strengths are those aspects of the organisation that it can build on whereas weaknesses are any deficiencies in the current levels of skills, resources, processes or organisation. The organisation needs to be aware of opportunities that are available in the environment in a number of different areas, for example market openings, products, social and economic developments. Threats are the other side of the coin and refer to any developments which may have an adverse impact on the organisation such as increased competition, changes in demand for products, legislative or economic developments which could affect demand, or changes to the industry infrastructure.

Companies will often seek to build on existing strengths or counteract weaknesses by acquiring or merging with other companies. For example, a manufacturing company might acquire a distribution firm to improve the quality of its product delivery. When two organisations merge the concept of synergy will be important. This means that the constituent parts should together form a whole greater than the sum of the individual parts. This is sometimes described as a situation in which 2 + 2 = 5.

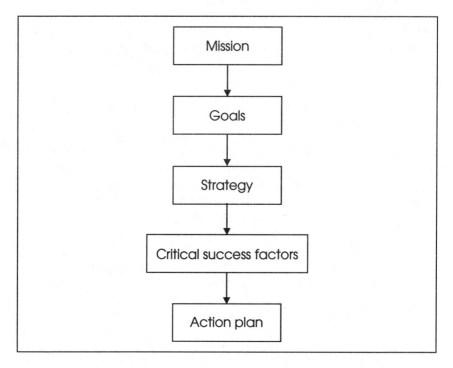

Figure 4.1   *The strategic planning process*

HOW GOOD ARE YOUR STRATEGIC OBJECTIVES?

The checklist below can be used to determine the effectiveness of your strategic objectives:

1. Do your objectives build on areas in which your organisation has distinctive strengths?
2. Are the objectives supported by key managers?
3. Are there both economic and non-economic objectives?
4. Are the objectives specific in terms of what must be delivered?
5. Do the objectives support the overall strategy of the organisation?

6. Are the objectives consistent?

7. Do the objectives have regard to the organisation's values?

Some of the other issues to be taken into account in determining corporate strategy are as follows:

- *Financial criteria* — in terms of the company's profitability, cash flow and time horizons.
- *Risk* — including:
  - the risk the company must accept;
  - the risk the company can afford to take;
  - the risk the company cannot afford to take;
  - the risk the company cannot afford not to take.
- *Personal values* — the organisation's ethics, the personal standards and values and their acceptability and credibility.
- *Internal consistency* — is the strategy consistent with the business mission and the company's defined policies, or does it conflict with other strategies?
- *Strategic balance* — is the organisation getting its strategy out of balance, ie depending too much on one area or moving too far from its main area of strength? Should the company 'stick to its knitting'?

CRITICAL SUCCESS FACTORS

In determining its strategic plan the organisation needs to pay attention to those factors which are critical if it is to achieve success. Any such factors must be dealt with effectively if the organisation is to achieve its mission and goals.

The following are common elements of critical success factors:

- *organisation characteristic* — eg price advantage, service type, service quality;
- *industry characteristic* — eg vertical integration, main competitors;
- *operating conditions* — eg capital structure, advantageous customer mix.

Critical success factors (CSFs) should help the organisation decide what the top management team should focus on to lead and direct the business and manage change. They should help to plan for major contingencies and determine the plans and actions required by the organisation to achieve its strategic objectives. CSFs assist in the identification of priorities for the allocation of resources, and identify the basic criteria for determining performance measures and incentives. They also assist in defining the appropriate organisation design.

Critical success factors may encompass, and should take account of, all the following elements:

- political;
- social;
- regulatory;
- financial;
- new discoveries and developments;
- market structure;
- competitors (actual and potential);
- pricing and cost structure;
- customer loyalty;
- specialisation;
- quality and quantity of supply;
- industrial climate;
- workforce;
- organisation.

Critical success factor checklist

The following checklist can be used to decide whether your critical success factors are appropriate:

- Is it generally agreed that all of the factors listed are critical to the success of the organisation and that any obstacles high-lighted must be overcome if the organisation is to achieve its mission and objectives?
- Is the top management team committed to dealing with all the factors?
- Are the factors listed comprehensive, ie do they all have to be dealt with if the organisation is to achieve its objectives?
- Is each critical success factor devoted only to one item?
- Is there a mix of short-term and long-term factors? If all the factors are short term there is a danger of leaving out long-term planning, and only long-term factors could mean that the organisation is not taking sufficient care of short-term aims.
- There should be no more than eight factors listed as it is usually unlikely for more than this number to be critical for the success of the organisation. Similarly, a larger number is liable to lead to a lack of focus in the organisation.

Examples of critical success factors

- **Brand image**
  Differentiate from competitors by providing superior quality.
- **Quality**
  Provide superior quality products and services.
- **New business opportunities**
  Keep ahead of competition by developing new products and pursuing new markets.
- **Human resources**
  Motivate and develop high quality staff.
- **Costs**
  Keep costs to levels lower than the competition.
- **Company image**
  Promote image as the leading supplier of core products.

ACTION PLANNING

Having decided on the organisation's overall objectives and agreed the factors that are critical to their attainment, the next step is to formulate detailed action plans to decide how the various factors are to be tackled and who is to be accountable.

Drawing up action steps

To draw up action steps the following processes should be used:

1. Imagine how the project should be undertaken, from start to finish.
2. Write down each task as it comes to mind and who will be involved, both in undertaking the task and providing the support.
3. Check that all tasks are included, and where possible use the MASTERS criteria to ensure that these tasks are:
   — Measurable;
   — Achievable;
   — Specific;
   — Time related;
   — Encompassing;
   — Realistic;
   — Stretching.
4. Clarify business assumptions that affect the work programme and the support required from others.

5. Arrange tasks in an appropriate sequence for the critical path, ie the tasks which are dependent on others being completed first.
6. Estimate the time required for each task, asking other people's views where appropriate.
7. Indicate the date and time for each task to begin and end.
8. Allocate the necessary resources for each task in terms of people, equipment, materials and other resources.
9. Agree with colleagues the appropriate review dates for reporting back on progress.

CONCLUSION

Much has been written on the concept of mission, especially since the mid 1980s. Some of the writing has concentrated heavily on the processes to put mission statements and organisational goals in place; others have concentrated on the outcomes and benefits from the culture change these processes are meant to induce. What needs to be borne in mind is that mission statements are intended to have two practical effects, the first internal, the second external.

Internally, mission statements, allied to achievable organisational goals and backed by clearly identified critical success factors, focus everyone's attention on where the company is going, how it is going to get there and what it needs to achieve. Put simply, mission statements can be a driving force if they are properly supported by managers at all levels and are realistic and achievable.

Externally, mission statements can be of considerable help in setting out the company's stall to its customers and the marketplace in general and in gaining the right customer focus and loyalty. Again they must be practical, or people will simply deride them, and realistic in terms of what the company can actually deliver.

Missionary zeal may have somewhat diminished since the late 1980s, but as a concept it still has a valuable place in most organisations, especially if it leads to clear thinking and action throughout.

References

[1]   Drucker, P (1968) *The Practice of Management*, Pan Books, London.
[2]   Campbell, A and Tawadey, K (1992) *Mission and Business Philosophy*, Butterworth-Heinemann, Oxford.

Organisation, Design and Structure

THE MEANING OF ORGANISATION STRUCTURE

An organisation's structure is the framework which explains how its resources are allocated and managed, and the lines of communication and decision making. These are usually shown as lines on an organisation chart, commonly called a 'family tree' or an 'organigram'. However, it is important to remember that lines drawn on paper in this way do not necessarily show how the organisation is actually structured, but rather the official view of the lines of communication and command.

This formal structure may be quite different from the informal structure. For example in Figure 5.1, while the official reporting line is from Job C to Job B, the reality may well be that the real communication and decision making takes place directly between A and C. The implications of this are discussed below.

The main purpose of the structure is to ensure that the organisation is designed in the best way to achieve its goals and objectives. In this sense all organisations, however small, have some kind of structure. If they did not, they would not be classified as organisations with a common purpose, but rather as loose groupings of individuals. While a structure therefore exists in organisations of all sizes, issues relating to its design only really become significant when a certain size and complexity are reached, although this can happen at a very early stage.

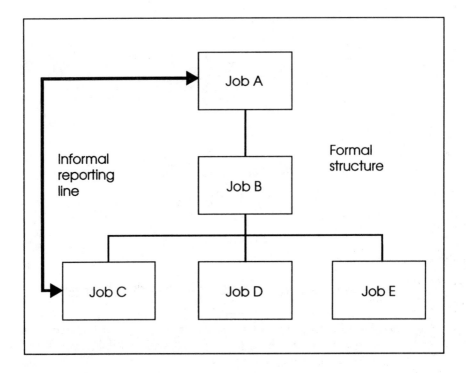

Figure 5.1   *Formal and informal reporting lines*

PURPOSES OF THE ORGANISATION STRUCTURE

An organisation's structure exists to achieve a number of purposes. These are to:

- support the organisation's strategy. The structure should be designed in such a way as to ensure the attainment of the organisation's goals and objectives. Strategy will be one of the main determinants of structure;
- organise resources in the most efficient and effective way;
- provide for the effective division of tasks and accountabilities among individuals and groups. Division in this way allows for specialisation within specific disciplines and activities, which becomes more essential as organisations grow in size and complexity;
- ensure effective coordination of the organisation's activities and clarify the decision-making processes;
- enhance and clarify the lines of communication up, down and across the organisation;

- allow for the effective monitoring and review of the organisation's activities;
- provide mechanisms for coping with change in markets, products and the internal and external environments;
- facilitate the handling of crises and problems;
- help to motivate, manage and give job satisfaction to individual members of the organisation;
- provide for management succession.

PRINCIPLES OF GOOD ORGANISATIONAL DESIGN

While it is difficult to be prescriptive about what constitutes a sound organisation structure, as this will depend on numerous characteristics individual to each organisation, there are a number of principles that tend to be common to the most effective structures. Before considering these principles, however, it needs to be stressed that organisations are only as effective as the people within them. While a good structure will improve the organisation's effectiveness, it is also true that even the best of structures will not work well unless the people in the organisation are appropriately motivated and trained.

The major principles of good organisational design may be broadly stated as follows:

1. Structure should follow strategy. The organisation and its various components should individually and collectively support the organisation's goals and objectives.
2. The various parts of the structure should be divided into specialist areas. This means that discrete areas of activity should be grouped together so that there can be a focus on specific objectives and a concentration of experience and expertise. Most commonly such specialisation is based on the different functions in the organisation, but there could also be multi-disciplinary groups divided on the basis of geography or product.
3. The number of levels in the structure, sometimes referred to as the scalar chain, should be as few as possible. The greater the number of levels within the structure, the more the problems of communication from top to bottom, of decision making, and of coordination and control.
4. The span of control, ie the number of subordinates directly managed, will vary according to the nature of the jobs and the organisation, but it should not be so narrow that it results in a

structure with too many levels, or too broad to allow effective management. Spans of control will vary greatly depending on the kind of jobs managed. A supervisor of manual workers might have 20 or 30 direct reports, whereas a director who is responsible for managers and professionals in different disciplines may only have three or four. As jobs increase in complexity they become consequently more difficult to manage.

While there is no magic formula for the ideal span of control, a larger number of direct reports will give a relatively flatter structure (see Figure 5.2). This has to be offset against the disadvantages involved in managing more direct subordinates and the greater difficulty in providing for succession to more senior posts.

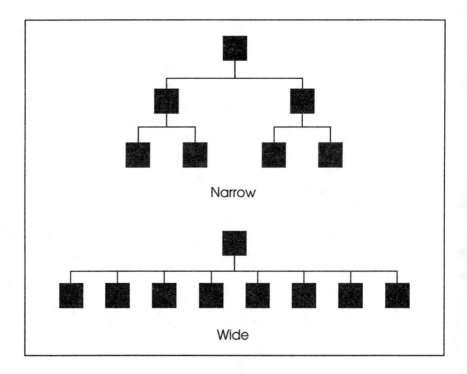

Figure 5.2   *Spans of control*

5. There should be what has been described as unity of command. In other words, there should be clarity about who each post holder reports to and who has the authority to take decisions.
6. Every post in the structure should have a clear role and add value to the way the organisation functions.
7. The extent to which the organisation should be centralised or decentralised will need to be determined by reference to a number of factors, including the nature and type of industry, geographical dispersion, history and so on.
8. The structure must be designed to take account of changes in the environment, which can include the economy, legislation, markets, technological developments, geography and so on. The main consideration is to develop a structure which is capable of accommodating change as it arises. Similarly, the structure should also provide for the training and development of future managers.

FACTORS AFFECTING ORGANISATION STRUCTURE

How an organisation is structured will depend on many factors. The most important of these are described below.

History

The organisation's present structure may have evolved over a number of years, as functions have been added, changed or deleted. Naturally, the older the organisation, the more important history is likely to be. It is also more likely to have determined the current structure if there have been relatively few pressures on the organisation to adapt to changing circumstances, either because it has monopolistic power or because the industry in which it operates is relatively slow moving. In the public sector, existing structures will usually be largely the result of past political and legislative changes.

Products and services

The kind of products or services provided by the organisation will affect its structure. For example, a manufacturing company may well have geographically dispersed plants with production lines, plus storage and warehousing facilities and a distribution network. In such an organisation the structure is likely to be based on the manufacturing process, with perhaps a number of different plants being run by separate managers, but with central coordination of the overall process. The complexity of a large-scale operation of this kind would be likely to mean that other aspects of the total process, such as distribution, sales and marketing, would be coordinated by different managers with overall coordination and control taking place at a relatively senior level. In this kind of organisation factors such as the availability of raw materials and skilled labour will be likely to affect the location of manufacturing plants.

Service organisations, on the other hand, will have different requirements and priorities and different functions. The line of communication between customer and service provider, for example, is likely to be much shorter than that between the manufacturer and the customer.

Where a range of products or services is being provided, the organisation may be structured around these different offerings. In a local authority, for example, there will usually be different departments for the functions of finance, planning, engineering, housing, environmental health and so on. While such groupings give the advantage of specialisation, they do create a degree of autonomy that can sometimes result in inter-departmental or inter-functional rivalry. This increases the need for effective coordination and control.

Customers and markets

The organisation structure will be affected by the type of market and customers it serves, and in a customer responsive environment this should be one of the main determinants of structure. If the organisation is providing services to a wide range of customers in a large number of locations, it may need to have numerous branch offices, as do banks, building societies, the Post Office and so on. Similarly, there may need to be product or service differentiation to cater for different types of customer or client. Larger management consultancies, for example, are sometimes organised on the basis of different market sectors so that there will be specialists in say the financial services and health sectors, the requirements of which are quite different.

Manufactured products will also be sold into markets that may have very different requirements. For example, selling cars to fleet buyers is likely to be a different process from selling to individuals. Overseas markets are also likely to require different specifications to products manufactured solely for the home market, as well as involving a different sales process.

Processes

The processes used within the organisation will also affect the structure. A production line process will consist of a number of separate tasks carried out by people specialising in those tasks at different stages of the process. The rationale behind this kind of approach is that specialisation means that people can develop high skills and speed, resulting in high output at low cost. There are of course disadvantages to this approach, primarily in terms of maintaining the motivation and morale of production line opera-tives. In contrast, social workers will usually have a case load and deal with a range of issues for a particular client, although the extent to which such jobs should be specialist or 'generic' is a matter of debate. Specialisation brings with it expertise but makes it more difficult to see the big picture and could result in conflicting decisions and approaches and lower flexibility.

People

People will affect an organisation structure in a number of ways. Firstly, structures do not just appear, they are the result of people's views and beliefs and their approach to managing the organisation. It is quite common, for example, for there to be posts within a structure which do not have a clearly defined role but which are there to accommodate people displaced after the last reorganisa-tion. The structure will also be affected by the types of jobs and people within the organisation. Structures with a large number of professionals are more likely to involve team working, and therefore to be relatively flat compared with an organisation that has to accommodate a range of jobs from the production line operative to the chairman.

Size

Perhaps the major influence on the structure of an organisation is its size. The larger the organisation, the greater the need for coordination of the various activities and for formal systems of communication and control. In such organisations there are more likely to be a number of specialist departments with coordination frequently taking place through meetings between departmental heads. The degree of formality is likely to increase directly in line with size. In large organisations issues of centralisation and decentralisation become very important.

Technology

Technology can have an impact on an organisation's structure in two ways. Firstly, the predominant technology with which the organisation is operating will affect the way work is done and how the organisation is structured. Secondly, the advent of new technology will continue to change working patterns. While in past years the staffing reductions projected owing to new technology did not arise, the result instead being increased numbers of information technology specialists within organisations, it does now appear that the point has been reached where numbers are falling because of the introduction of new technology. The reason for this apparent time lag may be that in the early stages the trend was to seek more information rather than reduce numbers.

Geography

The geographical dispersion of an organisation, perhaps because of the need to be near raw materials or customers, will affect its structure. Where there is a significant degree of geographical dispersion, for example numerous branch offices, there is likely to be more need for careful coordination and control than with a single site location.

THE DIFFERENT TYPES OF STRUCTURE

Organisations may be structured in a number of different ways and the most common of these are summarised below.

By function

One of the most usual approaches, especially in large organisations, is to group common activities together. For example, there may be separate departments for sales, production, finance, marketing and so on (see Figure 5.3). This gives the advantages that:

- the high degree of specialisation means that detailed experience and expertise can be developed in a specific area;
- there can be a clear focus on specific objectives relating to that function;
- the division of functions can act as a balancing mechanism so that there is less risk of policy being distorted by the dominance of one particular approach.

The disadvantages are that:

- it can encourage the growth of departmentalism which can act against the interest of the organisation as a whole;
- more coordination and control is needed over the various functions;
- it may slow down decision making and discourage innovation because of the difficulty of cutting across functional boundaries.

By geographical location

When there is a strong need to provide products or services within a particular geographical area, the organisation may be divided into regions or areas, with each being a fully self-contained, miniature version of the parent organisation (see Figure 5.4). The ideal size of geographical area for service provision is a matter of perennial debate within the public sector, particularly as the ideal size may be different for the provision of, say, education services, than for social services. In many cases, understanding the particular needs and requirements of the local area are of sufficiently fundamental importance for location to be the most significant factor in organisation design.

The advantages of a geographically based structure are:

- responsiveness to local needs;
- the ability to provide a complete service at one location;
- a degree of autonomy can provide for more efficient decision making and increase job satisfaction;
- the organisation can recruit locally based staff;
- it can facilitate the training and development of managers who can quickly gain varied experience in smaller branch offices before moving to larger jobs.

The disadvantages are that:

- it may be difficult to define the precise geographical area appropriate to the product or service in question;
- there is a need for careful coordination and communication to ensure that the various locations follow corporate strategy;
- a 'them and us' situation may be created, in which local managers resent what they regard as intrusion by the centre;
- it may be more difficult for locally based staff to gain recognition and climb the corporate ladder.

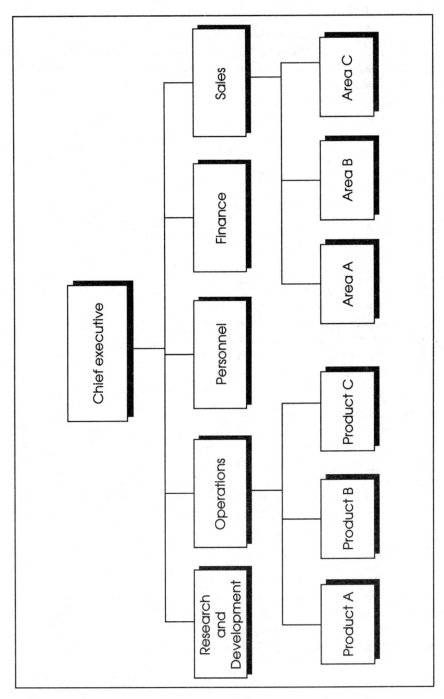

Figure 5.3   *A functional structure*

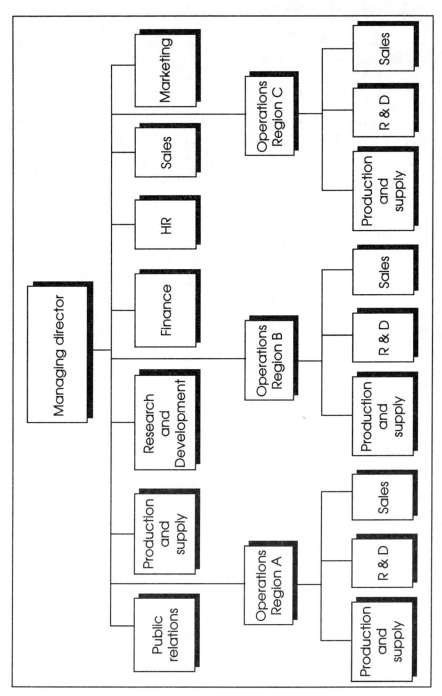

Figure 5.4 *A geographically based structure*

Products and services

The structure may be determined by the particular products and services provided (see Figure 5.5). Certainly in large and diverse organisations such as Grand Metropolitan, foods, hotels, and brewing are all separate divisions because they are dealing with very different products and services. Similarly, the Post Office has separate organisations for the various services it provides such as mail delivery (Royal Mail), parcel delivery (Parcelforce) and counter services (Post Office Counters Limited).

The advantages of product specialisation are that:

- it provides a focus on a specific area and encourages the development of expertise in the provision of that product or service;
- it is likely to provide a service that is more responsive to customer requirements;
- it is likely to be relatively self-contained

The disadvantages are that:

- too much focus on the product may overlook customers' real needs;
- it may not make the best use of the organisation's resources.

By processes and technology

The processes within the organisation might require the grouping together of certain activities, for example in a manufacturing environment where the different phases of the production process have to be grouped together. The technology will also affect the structure since an organisation which has a large number of relatively straightforward jobs, each perhaps carrying out routine and repetitive tasks, is likely to have managers with much wider spans of control than an organisation with large numbers of professional staff. In general terms, the greater the complexity of the job, the smaller the number of staff that can be effectively managed by one individual.

The advantages of organisation on the basis of process or technology are that:

- it allows for task specialisation which means that people can develop a high degree of skill;
- the emphasis on the outputs from a particular process can result in high productivity;

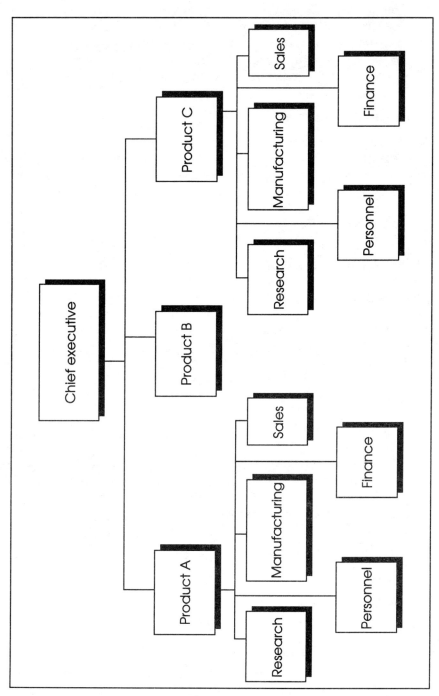

Figure 5.5 *A product based structure*

- the structure is easy to understand and manage and there is likely to be little ambiguity in the outputs to be achived;
- a structure that is driven by the organisation's processes is likely to require less supervisory input;
- processes that are particularly dirty, noisy or hazardous can be grouped together.

The main disadvantages are that:

- there is a danger that by concentrating on processes the organisation could lose sight of the inputs required;
- there is a greater need for the company's various processes to be integrated to ensure that they work towards the company's overall objectives;
- there is less focus on the customer.

By customers or clients

Organisation structures are determined by a number of factors and the all-important customer is too often left out of the equation. It is logical, however, for organisations to concentrate on the requirements of their customers. A good example is in the area of transportation, where clearly the emphasis will need to be on those routes which experience the heaviest demand. This will have to be counter-balanced by the need to provide a service over a full timetable, although it may mean at times that services are underutilised.

A customer focused structure can change the way things are done in the organisation in many ways. Above all, the organisation will require speedy and accurate feedback from its market and need the ability to respond flexibly to changes in trends and requirements. This means adapting the product to customers' requirements rather than trying to sell something that may not be entirely appropriate to their needs.

The advantages of a customer based structure (see Figure 5.6) are as follows:

- meeting customers' requirements is more likely to lead to long-term success for the organisation;
- it gives a clear focus to the organisation;
- it enables an emphasis to be put on the requirements of different customer groups, thereby improving overall service quality.

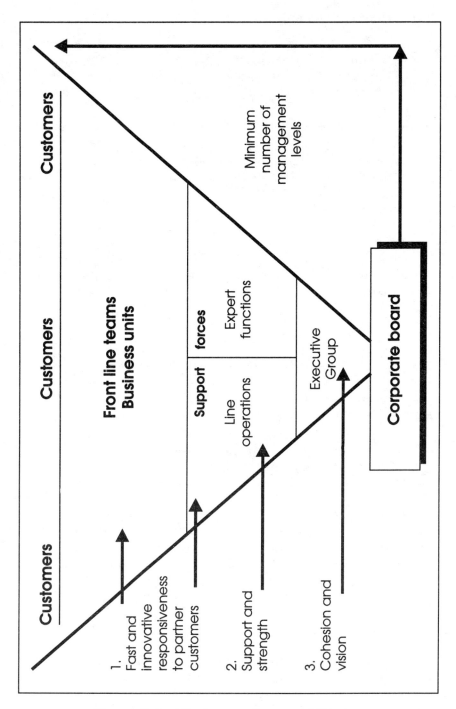

Figure 5.6   *The inverted pyramid (Hay)*

The main disadvantages are that:

- there is a need to keep a close eye on market requirements which could require a lot research;
- to be responsive to customer requirements the organisation needs to be very adaptable so that it can respond quickly to change;
- in many cases the provision of different services for different customer types may not allow for the most effective use of resources or for economies of scale;
- it may not always be economical or profitable for the organisation to provide some of the services required by customers, yet failure to do so will result in loss of goodwill;
- in some environments, the need to provide services outside normal working hours or around the clock will mean that shift working, stand-by and call-out arrangements will need to be introduced which will affect the way the organisation is structured.

Matrix structures

The types of organisation structure described above are the more traditional and stable ones, which may not be appropriate in organisations where the focus is on the delivery of professional services or specific projects. In an organisation providing professional services, for example a management consultancy or a law firm, there may be a need for specialists in a particular industry sector as well as specialists in particular disciplines. In this case the structure might look similar to that illustrated in Figure 5.7. In the same way, other organisations may require multi-disciplinary project teams, each of which have particular outputs to achieve, but requiring input from a range of different disciplines to achieve those objectives. An example is shown in Figure 5.8.

In matrix structures such as those described, traditional reporting lines tend to break down and teams might contain individuals from different levels in the organisation as well as from different disciplines. In some cases, the project manager might actually have a lower employment status than some members of the project team.

Typically where project teams are involved, staff may be seconded from other departments in the organisation to provide assistance with certain aspects of the project.

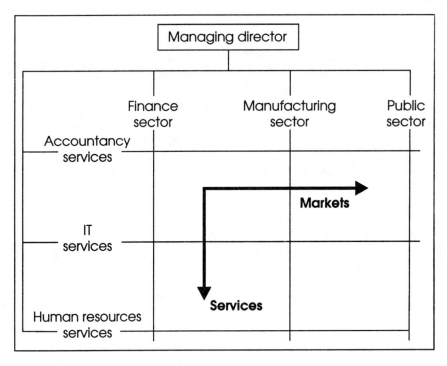

Figure 5.7 *A matrix structure in a consultancy*

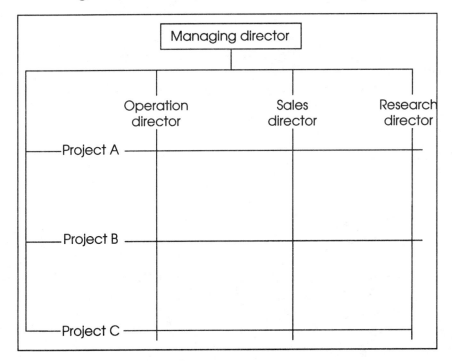

Figure 5.8 *A project-based matrix structure*

Matrix structures are appropriate where:

- the organisation is dealing with complex problems requiring a range of inputs from different disciplines;
- there is a need to subdivide the work of the organisation in more than one way, for example by industry and by function;
- when there is a substantial amount of information to be processed, for example on a police investigation.

The advantages of matrix structures are that:

- they are able to take advantage of a wide range of skills within the organisation;
- they offer an effective and flexible way of dealing with large amounts of data and complex problems;
- they can be focused on specific issues;
- they give considerable opportunities for the development of people within the organisation.

The main disadvantages of matrix structures are:

- they require a considerable amount of co-ordination and can result in large numbers of internal meetings;
- matrix structures are difficult to manage and can result in ambiguity about roles;
- there may be difficulty in defining the role of a project team and particularly of the project manager;
- there may be conflicting priorities between team members, departmental accountabilities and project team accountabilities;
- there can be difficulties in gaining the required degree of support from other parts of the organisation, resulting in tensions and conflicts;
- project teams can change the organisation structure and possibly be seen as undermining the authority of line managers.

COMMON PROBLEMS

Overlayering

A common problem, particularly in larger organisations, is over-layering or having too many levels in the structure. This leads to extended lines of decision making with the consequence that the organisation is unable to respond quickly to developments. Vertical communication also becomes more difficult and the posts at the top of the structure become out of touch with those at the bottom. Tall structures of this kind are likely to be less cost effective because of the additional staff roles that are required.

There are many factors which affect the number of levels including, for example, spans of control (see below), making over-fine distinctions between different sizes of job, the range and type of jobs, the organisation's history and even the grade structure.

In considering whether or not the number of levels is correct the key questions that managers should ask are: 'What value do these jobs contribute to the organisation?' and 'What would happen if these jobs did not exist?'

Too few levels

The less common converse of having too many levels is having too few. This can often occur as a result of trying to avoid the problems referred to above. While the advantages of a relatively flat structure are improved communication and faster, more responsive decision making, there are also a number of disadvantages.

Firstly, having too few levels is likely to mean that spans of control are too wide with managers having more direct reports than they can effectively co-ordinate. This is particularly so where a variety of functions are involved.

Secondly, there will inevitably be a wide difference between the scope of a particular management post and the posts reporting to it. This could cause problems in succession planning as the more specialised posts in the lower tiers would be unlikely to have the necessary breadth to be able to undertake the more senior role. It may also be difficult to find someone with the knowledge and experience to fill a post with such wide-ranging accountabilities.

Finally, there is the danger of departmentalism, in which particular departments or functions pursue their own narrow interests which may not be consistent with those of the organisation.

Inappropriate span of control

The span of control refers to the number of direct subordinates controlled by a manager and this will have a direct impact on the number of organisational levels.

It is sometimes suggested that there is an ideal span of control. However, while wide spans of control will reduce the number of tiers in the structure, it is an over-simplification to suggest that there should, for example, be a minimum span of five direct reports. One organisation adopted this kind of approach to the letter and this led to the spectacle of managers creating posts to achieve their required number of subordinates.

Some major research in this area was carried out by Woodward,[1] whose study of 100 manufacturing firms in Essex found a wide variety of spans of control, which varied with the technology and production systems in use. On the whole, however, there was little direct correlation between what were regarded as the rules of management and business success.

The reality is that there is no magic formula. The most appropriate span of control will depend on a number of factors, including:

- the type of organisation;
- the complexity of the organisation and the technology involved;
- the abilities of managers and subordinates;
- the range of activities carried out and their diversity or homogeneity;
- the type of work;
- number and geographical location of offices, plants and so on;
- the quality of the organisation's co-ordination and control mechanisms;
- organisation culture and managerial preferences.

One over one

Of course the smallest span of control is where there is one post in direct line with another, frequently as a deputy. The question which then has to be asked is what value is being added to the organisation by both posts. Such an arrangement should generally be viewed with suspicion, although it can be justified where there is a clear division of accountabilities and focus, and particularly where it is necessary for the organisation to have a figurehead whose focus is primarily external.

Overlapping or missing accountabilities

Any structure should be designed to ensure that all required organisation functions are carried out and that there is no duplication. Overlaps in accountabilities occur when more than one person is held responsible for the same outputs. This usually occurs horizontally across the structure but it can also happen vertically. Obviously such duplication is wasteful and inefficient and causes confusion.

Missing accountabilities can arise when no one is held responsible for specific outputs, in which case there is a good chance they will not be achieved.

Unclear reporting lines

People need to be clear about who they report to, otherwise the organisation will be unable to manage performance effectively. Unclear or multiple reporting lines make it difficult for individuals to be clear about their objectives, especially when those they are reporting to have different priorities.

Confusion about reporting lines can particularly occur when a postholder has both line and functional accountabilities. For example, in a large organisation there might be a central personnel function but also personnel officers in a number of separate departments. In such a situation it is common for the departmental personnel officer to report directly to the department manager, who would be his or her line manager for matters such as discipline, performance appraisal and welfare, but also to retain a functional link to the central personnel function for advice and guidance on human resources policy.

Further confusion can arise when particular staff roles are carried out at the centre on behalf of senior executives. Such roles can give individuals authority over other people in the organisation, even though they have no direct line responsibility. Where such influence is exercised without going through the line manager it can lead to tension.

These kinds of staff role need to be distinguished from those typically found in an organisation, such as legal, finance, personnel and other non-line roles. These people will not usually be directly involved in line management as their roles are predominantly advisory in nature.

Too much centralisation or decentralisation

A common dilemma in organisations is the extent to which activities should be controlled from the centre. The extent of centralisation that is appropriate will depend on the size and complexity of the organisation, the geographical spread and the preferences of the managers.

The main advantages of centralisation are that:

- it is easier for the organisation to develop a corporate strategy and implement common objectives;

- there is likely to be more consistency and faster decision making;
- overall co-ordination and control are likely to be easier;
- economies of scale are more likely to be achieved;
- there is less likelihood of functions being duplicated;
- independent empires are less likely to be created;
- a strong central organisation can provide a pool of expertise and specialist advice for the rest of the organisation.

The main disadvantages are that:

- too much co-ordination and control can undermine the authority of managers at the 'sharp end' and damage morale;
- when decisions are taken too far away from the operational base they may not accurately reflect reality;
- it can discourage managers from taking decisions at the local level;
- once organisations reach a certain size, or when they are widely dispersed geographically, co-ordination is likely to become more difficult with the consequent danger of staff jobs and internal controls proliferating;
- managers are unlikely to gain the experience necessary to enable them to develop into more senior posts;
- locally based services are more likely to be able to respond speedily and accurately to local demand;
- Centralised organisations can become inflexible and bureaucratic, with the consequence that local managers may decide to go their own way.

Clearly the advantages of centralisation are the disadvantages of decentralisation and vice versa. However, probably the biggest disadvantage of a structure that is too decentralised is that the various separate divisions, departments and so on are likely to pursue their own agendas which may not support the corporate strategy.

Ambiguity in matrix structures and project teams

One of the most difficult types of structure to manage is the matrix. This is frequently used when a number of different product types are being sold to a variety of markets. The main difficulties are likely to be deciding where the main focus should be and ensuring that there is good communication across the structure.

Project teams whose members hold a variety of posts, and which often have people at different levels in the organisation, can lead to confusion about reporting lines and difficulty in deciding priorities.

EFFECTS OF POOR ORGANISATION STRUCTURE

While it is probably true to say that well motivated and high performing employees will usually succeed despite a poor organisation structure, such a structure would be likely to have the following consequences:

- poor motivation and morale;
- ineffective decision making;
- a lack of co-ordination and control;
- no adherence to corporate objectives;
- poor communication;
- divisiveness and lack of co-operation, with everyone trying to protect their own domains;
- higher costs and inefficiency;
- an inability to respond effectively to changing conditions or to innovate;
- duplication of certain activities and possibly failure to undertake others;
- failure to provide suitable opportunities for the development of future managers.

References

[1] Woodward, J (1980) *Industrial Organisation: Theory and Practice*, Oxford University Press, Oxford.

Jobs and Roles

All organisations exist for a purpose or to achieve a mission (see Chapter 4), and to achieve that purpose or mission they have to carry out a number of different tasks. These tasks or groups of tasks form the basis of the jobs or posts within the organisation.

It follows that for an organisation to be successful all it has to do is find people with the necessary skills and knowledge to undertake the jobs in question. However, things are never quite that simple. One of the problems, which increases with the difficulty of the job, is finding people who will produce the required results without in the process changing the job. Every individual will do the same job in a different way, which in turn changes the job.

One of the key issues to be dealt with by any organisation, therefore, is the extent to which it should try to separate the job from the person. If the organisation is to achieve its objectives it is vital for it to have jobs described in objective terms with clearly defined outputs.

On the other hand, the organisation has to ensure that its employees are motivated and that it takes advantage of individual skills and abilities. In essence, this means ensuring not only that jobs are clearly defined, but also that individual abilities are, as far as possible, recognised, measured and developed. People will inevitably change their jobs, but at the same time it must be clear to them that there are certain key outputs which they are required to achieve or their performance will not be regarded as entirely satisfactory.

This chapter deals with the above issues and considers in particular:

- the analysis of jobs and preparation of job descriptions;
- jobs and roles;
- the design of jobs.

JOB ANALYSIS

Job analysis is the process of gathering factual information about a job. This information should be presented in such a way that it communicates an instant understanding of what the job is about. The output from job analysis is usually in the form of a job description.

People hold a variety of views about the value of job descriptions, ranging from those who consider them to be completely unnecess-ary to those who feel they cannot do their jobs without them. Both these extremes follow from over-rigid application of job descrip-tions. People should not be able to refuse to carry out certain activities 'because they are not in my job description', nor should managers use job descriptions in an arbitrary or authoritarian way. In contrast job descriptions should set out the key results to be achieved in a job which should also be discussed with the individual post holder. The format of the job description is described in more detail below.

THE USES OF JOB DESCRIPTIONS

Job descriptions have many uses, including:

- *job evaluation* — to enable the organisation to place a value on the job according to its relative size;
- *organisation analysis* — to ensure that all the organisation's activities are covered and that there are no serious omissions or duplications;
- *human resource planning* — to assist in identifying the numbers and types of jobs required;
- *recruitment and selection* — to assist in determining the knowledge, skills and experience required to undertake the job effectively;
- *training and development* — to assist in identifying any areas of knowledge, skills or experience that need to be enhanced;
- *performance management* — to assist in identifying the outputs to be achieved which can then be translated into individual targets.

It is worth distinguishing between the job description, which sets out the activities within the post, and the personnel specification, which outlines the characteristics required of the individual filling the post, for example qualifications and years of experience required, skills necessary and personal attributes.

TYPES OF JOB DESCRIPTION

Job descriptions can take many different forms and there will, for example, be significant differences between a task based job description for a routine operational job and that for a professional or managerial post. For the latter kinds of job the description will need to be written more in terms of outputs rather than the specific tasks to be carried out (see examples below).

Example of a task based job description

Job title: Accounts Clerk
Job number: 1235
Name of job holder:
Reports to: Senior Accountant
Date: 1 June 1993

Main Purpose of Job

To undertake routine clerical duties in support of an accounting function.

Main Activities

1. Process payments and invoices in accordance with closely defined procedures.
2. Verify calculations and input computer codes for a variety of documents.
3. Check ledgers, statements and accounts to identify errors and take any necessary corrective action, referring more complex items to the supervisor.
4. Respond to customer enquiries and complaints, by telephone or in writing, after having checked the relevant facts from existing records.
5. Carry out any statistical analysis as required.
6. Draft any routine correspondence.
7. Undertake routine administrative support procedures such as assisting with filing, opening post, etc.

Skill and Experience Requirements

This job requires previous experience in an accounts office and a sound understanding of office procedures. Normal entry requirements will be 4 GCSE passes at Grade C and above including English and Maths. An accurate and analytical mind and good telephone skills are required. The post holder may also need to operate a VDU terminal to input or access information.

Example of an accountability based job description

Job title:	Director of Marketing	Signed:
Job holder:		Job holder:
Reports to:	Chief Executive	Date:

Main Purpose of Job

To develop current business, identify new initiatives and funding sources and to ensure the effective development and promotion of the company and its products.

Principal Accountabilities

1. Identify and develop new initiatives to improve the range and quality of the products provided by the company and to ensure responsiveness to changes in the external environment.
2. Develop all necessary policies and approaches to ensure the effective promotion and marketing of the company.
3. Analyse trends in the business environment, help to develop products that are responsive to identified demands, and identify new market opportunities.
4. Assist in formulating and monitoring the annual business plan to ensure the long-term success and viability of the company and the attainment of corporate objectives.
5. Critically evaluate the costs and benefits of all new ideas and initiatives to ensure that resources are appropriately directed and to keep the company ahead of its competitors.
6. Direct and control the staff of the directorate to ensure that they are appropriately motivated and trained and are working towards the achievement of the company's corporate objectives.
7. Advise the company, as part of the corporate management team, on the development of new initiatives and the promotion and marketing of products to ensure the achievement of the company's business plan and corporate objectives.
8. Control and monitor the directorate's finances to ensure effective budgeting and cost control.

The purpose for which the job description is to be used will be a key determinant of the way it is written. For example, it is very common to see job descriptions which describe the activities carried out by a particular post rather than the outputs to be achieved. While such descriptions are very useful in terms of indicating to post holders the actions they are required to take — particularly valuable for induction purposes — they are not adequate to give a full understanding of the job.

CONTENT OF THE JOB DESCRIPTION

Essential information

Any job description should contain as a minimum the following:

1. Name of organisation.
2. Department or section.
3. Title of job.
4. Name of job holder (this may need to be left out in certain circumstances, particularly when a post is being evaluated and anonymity is required to encourage objectivity).
5. Job code or post number (where applicable).
6. Date (essential as jobs can change very quickly).
7. A summary of the main purpose of the job.
8. A description of the main accountabilities or duties of the job, preferably including an indication of the approximate percentage of time spent on each.
9. An indication of any specific requirements relating to the post, eg skills required, environmental conditions.
10. Reporting relationships, particularly in terms of who the post holder reports to and the numbers and types of direct and indirect subordinates. (This may be supported or replaced by an attached organisation chart.)
11. Any dimensions or statistics relating to the job, eg budgets managed, forms processed.
12. Signature of post holder and post holder's boss to indicate that the job description has been agreed.

The following additional information may also be desirable:

1. Job context — the environment in which the job is carried out and how it relates to the overall work of the organisation and department.
2. Decision making — the limits of authority of the job, including examples of the kinds of decision that may have to be referred upwards and the main rules, policies and procedures to be followed.
3. Communication and contacts — the main lines of communication and contact both within and outside the organisation.
4. Jobs of subordinates — brief descriptions of the jobs carried out by the post holder's subordinates.
5. Working relationships — describing the way in which decisions, objectives and results are communicated upwards and downwards.

6. Problems and challenges — the most challenging aspects of the job and kinds of problems dealt with.
7. Examples of work or projects carried out by the post holder.
8. Additional information — any extra information that either the post holder or the boss feels should be included.

Features of a good job description

A good job description is one in which:

- the job content is up to date and accurate;
- the job title is appropriate to the main purpose of the job;
- the main purpose or job summary accurately encapsulates in one or two sentences the principal reason why the job exists;
- the main tasks or accountabilities are not too detailed (for example, Hay Management Consultants Ltd generally takes the view that for professional and managerial jobs there should be a list of no more than eight principal accountabilities which should each describe what the post holder does, why he or she does it, and the end result);
- there is sufficient information for the reader with no prior knowledge of the job to gain a complete and accurate understanding of what the job entails (sufficient to be able to evaluate it if required);
- information is presented consistently.

ANALYSING A JOB AND PREPARING A JOB DESCRIPTION

There are a number of ways of gathering information about jobs. The principal ways are:

1. *Observation* — particularly appropriate for manual operations.
2. *Interviewing the post holder* — this should be the best source of information as no one is likely to know the job better.
3. *Interviewing the post holder's boss* — particularly where there is no one currently occupying the post being reviewed.
4. *Preparing a job description questionnaire* — normally completed by the post holder and countersigned by the boss.

Probably the most effective means of undertaking a thorough job analysis exercise is as follows:

- design a questionnaire to obtain the required information (structured questionnaires with different sections are necessary to ensure consistency of information);

- ask post holders to complete the questionnaires in draft;
- interview the post holders to ensure that the information provided is accurate and comprehensive;
- prepare a polished version of the job description;
- discuss the polished job description with the post holder's boss, make any final adjustments and obtain the boss's agreement to the final version.

Where this process involves the analysis of a large number of jobs, as in a major job evaluation exercise, some stages may have to be curtailed. Whichever approach is adopted, however, the final job description should be one which is agreed by both the post holder and his or her boss. Where there are a number of similar posts, it may be desirable to compare a number of job descriptions prepared by different post holders and to produce one composite version.

As an alternative to the questionnaire and interview approach, there are in existence a number of computer-based job analysis programmes. These operate by describing a number of different skill areas or behavioural competences, and inviting the system user to select the description which is most appropriate to the job in question. A complete picture of the job can be built up. The selection of the different levels and headings can be carried out by the post holder, subject to checking and verification by his or her boss.

Principles of job analysis

In analysing jobs the following principles should be adhered to:

1. The analyst must seek to understand exactly what the job is about, including the actions that are taken and the reasons for those actions. The aim is to produce a comprehensible job description which communicates understanding of the job rather than a mere list of tasks.

2. The final job description should relate only to those tasks and functions that are part of the job. The impact of the individual on the job has, as far as possible, to be ignored. Where an item is not being carried out by a post holder, perhaps because he or she does not have the necessary skills or experience, but it is still part of the job, it should be included. Similarly, where an individual is undertaking activities that are beyond the scope of the job as described, perhaps because he or she is particularly adept, these should not form part of the job description unless it is officially recognised by the organisation that the job has changed to include them. The analysis is of the job, not the person.

3. It is not the role of the analyst to make judgements about the job, but just to convey a full and accurate description.
4. Job descriptions should reflect the current position and not anticipate changes that may not take place, or include out-of-date information.

ROLES AND JOBS

An understanding of role theory is valuable for analysing the behaviour of individuals in an organisation. In general terms an individual's role comprises the pattern of behaviour demonstrated by that person and which has a particular predictable outcome. A certain pattern of behaviour is expected from a particular role, for example we would expect our mother to behave in a particular way most of the time.

In an organisation people are assigned roles according to their position in the hierarchy. Someone occupying a particular position would be expected to behave in a certain way by those they interact with (known as their role-set) and would themselves develop their own perception of how they should behave in a particular role.

People may or may not conform to others' expectations. Where they do not, conflicts or misunderstandings can arise. For example, subordinates may have a perception of the managerial role which differs from the way the manager sees the job.

There are certain expectations about particular roles and often these produce similar patterns of behaviour. It would be expected, for example, that all managers would dress formally, be punctual and set an example. People in any particular role-set or category, that is, grouped with other people in similar roles, might be expected to base their behaviour patterns on what they would regard as successful role models, those whose success is achieved by conforming to certain standards and types of behaviour.

ROLE CONFLICT AND AMBIGUITY

Everyone undertakes a number of different roles in life. For example, any one person might be at the same time a son, a father, an employee, treasurer of the local golf club, a committee member, and so on. All these roles call for different behaviours and arouse different expectations in others. This is carried over into the workplace. A first-line supervisor, for example, is the boss of those he or she supervises, but the subordinate of the person above. The individual may be required on the one hand to represent the views of operatives to management but on the other hand implement management policy. Jobs are frequently filled by individuals who are promoted from the workforce they have to supervise. This can be a very difficult transition, as the desire to remain part of the work group is likely to conflict with the need to exert discipline. Role conflict can easily arise in such situations. The contradictory expectations of workers and managers can place the first-line supervisor in an unenviable position.

Role ambiguity arises when the post holder is unclear about what is expected. Often it may not be clear, for example, exactly what the limitations of an individual's authority are. Sometimes managers even leave precise accountabilities deliberately vague, but this is not a course to be recommended as it is likely to make effective performance difficult.

ROLE OVERLOAD AND ROLE UNDERLOAD

Role overload arises when a person has too many roles to carry out or is trying to meet too many expectations. For example, combining a job with a strong planning and developmental aspect with one that also has to deal with a variety of day-to-day, short-term, urgent problems is likely to lead to conflict in determining priorities. An example of this might be combining a training and development role with one dealing with recruitment and conditions of service in a large organisation. Similarly, where someone is reporting to more than one person each one may have different expectations and there are likely to be occasional conflicts of priorities.

Role underload can arise when someone is not being used as fully as his or her experience and abilities could allow. This is likely to lead to frustration and demotivation for the person concerned.

WAYS OF REDUCING ROLE CONFLICT AND STRESS

Role conflict of the kind described above is clearly undesirable and may be reduced in a number of ways. These include:

- designing jobs carefully and producing clear job descriptions;
- having clear policies and procedures;
- having clear personnel specifications which ensure, as far as possible, that people appointed match the requirements of the job in question;

- Effective management of performance, particularly including counselling and coaching by line managers;
- identifying training needs clearly and providing appropriate training and development;
- redesigning jobs where necessary to reduce (or increase) the number of roles undertaken;
- clarifying organisational objectives and individual targets;
- Ensuring that the organisation structure and processes are appropriate, for example clear lines of accountability and reasonable spans of control;
- Ensuring that managerial and supervisory staff are aware of the symptoms of stress.

TRANSACTIONAL ANALYSIS

One approach that can help in understanding organisational roles is transactional analysis, developed by Berne.[1] According to this theory, each individual has three ego states that exist simultaneously. These are described as the adult, parent and child ego states. These ego states are characterised by Berne as:

- *adult* — an aspect of the personality which is primarily engaged in rational and reasoning thought;
- *child* — an aspect of the personality which functions in a childlike way, for example playing, being disruptive, or using the imagination;
- *parent* — an aspect of the personality which behaves in a parental way, by criticising or nurturing, and so on.

In interpersonal communications these ego states can have positive or negative consequences. For example, if one person adopts a childlike response to adult behaviour, by behaving playfully to someone seeking information or carrying out logical reasoning, this may be badly received. Equally, where someone adopts a critical parent stance, this will be effective as long as the other person behaves as a compliant child. On the other hand, the reaction may be the negative one of a disruptive child.

Clearly, interpersonal communication will be effective where the respective roles adopted are compatible. Where, for example, one person plays the role of parent, this means the other will have to be content to undertake the child role if communication is to be effective. By the same token, it would be expected that most transactions in organisations would be adult to adult (see Figure 6.1).

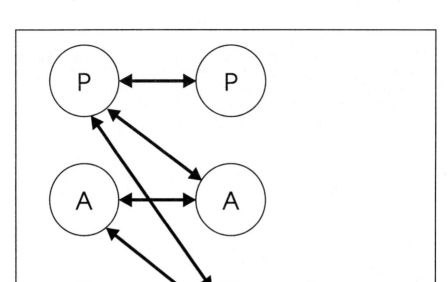

Figure 6.1   *Role combinations in transactional analysis*

JOB DESIGN

The issue of job design cannot really be separated from that of motivation and this chapter should therefore be read in conjunction with Chapter 8.

Effective job design will mean different things in different organisations and for white-collar and blue-collar jobs. In many organisations, particularly where manufacturing processes are involved, there may be little scope for redesigning jobs. The demands of the processes might mean that jobs have to be broken down into relatively small components. This is the principle of task specialisation, which is based on the assumption that greater efficiency come from people concentrating on one particular activity at which they can become very skilled.

While there is little doubt that the constant repetition of straightforward activities will lead to high levels of skill and speed in those activities, the major problem is the likelihood of boredom and lack of challenge. This has been one of the main arguments against the division of labour in this way and has led, in the past, to the development of group technology. For example, in the car industry a team of workers makes the entire vehicle rather than carrying out one specific activity at a particular stage of the production process.

The group technology approach has been successfully adopted by Volvo, where the workers are organised into self-regulating teams responsible for the assembly of complete subsections. The teams elect their own leaders and distribute work in the way that best suits them. This is claimed to have resulted in significant improvements in levels of absenteeism and productivity over the years.

There is also of course, a significant amount of task specialisation in white-collar jobs, but these perhaps have more scope for being changed or extended because they are less likely to be dependent on the high level of physical dexterity that task specialisation develops.

Factors leading to job satisfaction

There are a number of factors that can lead to increased job satisfaction. Some of these are intrinsic to the work itself, whereas others relate to external rewards. The intrinsic factors include the following:

1. *Variety* — while concentration on one particular task might lead to high levels of skill and efficiency, it is likely to prove very boring. Boredom can lead to errors, a lack of motivation and high levels of absenteeism. One of the factors that is likely to improve job satisfaction is building some variety into the work undertaken.
2. *Control over the work* — the degree of satisfaction experienced by a person will be affected by the degree of freedom over the work being carried out and the scope to make decisions about it.
3. *Task relevance* — people will only be motivated to the extent that they feel the task they are carrying out is of significance to the organisation and that they can see how it fits in with the overall process;
4. *Feedback on results* — the degree of job satisfaction will depend on the amount of feedback people get about their performance, particularly the extent to which they might be praised for doing a good job.
5. *Personal growth* — the extent to which an individual feels the job will help develop skills and knowledge.

Implications for job design

From the above it should be clear that as far as possible jobs should:

- provide variety in terms of the kind of work carried out, its pace, location etc;
- allow people to get direct feedback on results;
- allow scope for development by enabling the job to become bigger as the person becomes more skilled and knowledgeable;
- have clear objectives and outputs;
- have clear reporting lines;
- give people some control over output and pace;
- give people the opportunity to comment on and suggest changes to the work process;
- be supported by the appropriate level of resources and effective processes.

REDESIGNING JOBS

In considering the design of jobs in an organisation, account needs to be taken of the following:

1. *The volume of work*, which will determine overall numbers of jobs. For this reason the first step will need to be an assessment of workload.
2. *The complexity of the work* to be undertaken, both in terms of its variety or breadth and its technical difficulty or depth. Clearly there may be a need to distinguish between jobs or tasks that are of a professional or managerial nature, those that are technical and those that are routine or clerical.
3. *The work processes involved.* It might be desirable for one person to be involved in an entire process, or the work flows may be such that this is not practical and the process has to be split between several different people.
4. *The nature of the people currently employed* in the organisation. While many jobs contain a mixture of the routine and the more complex, not everyone is able to cope with a variety of different tasks and different levels of work. The extent to which jobs can be redesigned will therefore depend largely on the kind of people employed. This will also have an impact on the kind of flexibility that might be possible. If the aim is to introduce a multi-skilled team, this is dependent on having people who can cope with that flexibility and the ambiguity that can also arise.

5. *The sequence of flows in the process.* The sequence of events and their timings will affect how the work can be organised. Where activities are carried out over a longer period, this is likely to entail greater complexity.
6. *The timescales.* Where instant responses are required, specific jobs may have to be earmarked to provide such responses. Work requiring longer planning horizons is likely to be more complex and needs therefore to be done at a higher level. It should also be borne in mind that more routine, day-to-day and immediate work tends to take priority over longer-term developmental activities which might, as a consequence, not be completed as quickly as they should.
7. *The geographical dispersion of the organisation's activities.* Where, for example, there are a number of different locations, there may be a need to cover a whole range of activities which would otherwise have been grouped together in one place. It is often the case that people working in small offices geographically remote from a larger centre gain a greater variety of experience in a shorter space of time.
8. *The involvement of other parts of the organisation* in the overall process. There may be a need for extensive communication and co-ordination and the design of jobs should take account of the way this is to be achieved.
9. *The impact of information technology.* There may be wide scope for changing the way work is done and also the information that is provided. Similarly, there may be the opportunity for much more flexible working arrangements, such as 'telecommuting' where individuals provide a service to the organisation via a home based computer terminal.

CONCLUSION

There are many ways in which jobs may be redesigned to make them more interesting and flexible. This is important because not only will more interesting jobs provide greater job satisfaction and therefore be likely to reduce absenteeism and improve motivation, but also greater flexibility means that the organisation can more effectively cover peaks in workload or reduction in staff resources. It might also enable the organisation to develop its own managers and provide more effective goods and services.

However, it is not just the work content and the way the job is designed that will influence people. They will also be concerned — perhaps more concerned — about their pay, conditions of service, working environment, relationships with colleagues, the culture and climate of the organisation, relationships with the boss and so on. This all relates to the field of motivation which is considered in more depth in Chapter 8.

References

1   Berne, E (1963) *The Structure and Dynamics of Organizations and Groups*, Grove Press, New York.

Teams and Groups

T he aim of this chapter is to define what is meant by groups and to examine the factors which determine their effectiveness.

DEFINITION

A work group or team is a collection of people with a common purpose who:

- interact with each other;
- are psychologically aware of each other;
- perceive themselves to be a group.

The above definition is useful because it characterises a group of people who would probably describe themselves in terms of 'we'. In other words, membership of a particular department or function in an organisation does not necessarily mean that people are part of a group or team, although they may well interact and have a common purpose.

Groups and teams are formed in organisations to carry out specific roles, but will also emerge naturally where there are people with common interests.

FORMAL AND INFORMAL GROUPS

Formal groups are those that are deliberately created within the organisation for a specific purpose. They will have nominated leaders, defined functions to perform and, usually, clearly determined ways of carrying out their activities. Such formal groups may be arranged to carry out a particular task, or to cover a particular area of work, or because of their particular status or level within the organisation, such as a senior management cadre. Such groups will normally have clear rules and will be officially recognised by managers who will impose controls on their activities.

In contrast, all organisations will also have informal groups. These will be established by people who feel they have common interests which may be additional to or different from those of the formal groups. They may simply be groups of people who find that they are able to work well together. Such informal groups will normally cut across organisational reporting lines and have the potential to be disruptive if the interests of group members are different from those of the formal organisation. On the other hand, such groups will inevitably form and can be very beneficial if their aims are in support of the organisation's objectives. However, the main reason that people belong to these groups is for their own personal satisfaction.

GROUP NORMS

All groups produce their own norms of behaviour, shared perceptions of how things should be done or a common attitude to particular circumstances. These standards or patterns of behaviour are what create the group's identity, and there can be substantial pressure to conform to them. The norms themselves can relate to all kinds of activities including the pace of work (a common situation where group bonuses are involved), the quality of work done and relationships with other groups and individuals.

These group pressures can be very strong, and the more people identify with a particular group, the more likely they are to adhere to the group norms.

GROUP COHESIVENESS

Cohesiveness means the ability of the group to withstand pressure from outside. Some groups, for example, may be a loose and fragmented affiliation, whereas others may be very closely integrated and difficult to enter or break down. Where group members are loyal and strongly support the goals of the group it may be described as highly integrated.

GROUP FORMATION

There are a number of factors affecting group formation, probably the most important of which is physical proximity. A powerful combination of factors occurs when people are thrown together in one location and under stress. Even in situations such as hostage taking, the victims and the aggressors can tend to think of themselves as one group after a period of time. The other factors affecting group formation are:

- mutual attraction, when people group together because of their liking for each other;
- the need to co-operate to achieve a common objective;
- personal gains to be derived from belonging to a particular group, such as gaining information or contacts;
- the need for emotional support, particularly at times of stress.

Factors affecting the way the group behaves are such things as:

- size of group;
- age, sex and social background of members;
- time period over which the group is formed, for example on a training course;
- perceived rewards from group membership;
- group leadership.

It is widely believed that groups go through four stages of development.[1] These are commonly described as follows:

1. *Forming*. At this stage the group members find out about each other, and the structure and rules of the group begin to be determined. There is likely to be a lot of silence and anxiety from group members as they seek to find their role within the group and clarify its nature.
2. *Storming*. This is a stage at which arguments and conflicts arise as people seek to establish themselves within the group. They are likely to search for ideas, gather information and test and develop opinions. This can be a noisy and emotional phase.
3. *Norming*. At this stage the initial conflicts are resolved and there is a more open exchange of ideas and views. Group co-operation builds up and individual group roles are clarified. There is a growth of cohesiveness within the group and agreement about group norms.
4. *Performing* This is the stage at which the group focuses on problem solving and outputs with a higher degree of energy and commitment to reach decisions acceptable to all group members.

HIGHLY COHESIVE GROUPS AND THE DANGER OF GROUP THINK

While highly cohesive groups will normally exhibit high morale and productivity, there are dangers. Irving Janis[2] gives a number of historical examples where highly cohesive groups made what were in some cases disastrous decisions because of that very cohesiveness. One example quoted is that of the Bay of Pigs fiasco when the United States backed an abortive invasion of Cuba. At the time there was strong evidence that the President was surrounded only by people who reinforced his own views and any opposing ones were effectively screened out by self-appointed 'mind guards'. This is a graphic illustration of how unwilling such tightly knit groups can be to countenance any views other than their own. There can be a tendency to disregard and underestimate outsiders, particularly opposition groups. The cohesiveness of any group will be affected by a number of factors, including:

- *frequency of meeting* — the more frequently the members meet the greater the group's cohesiveness will become;
- *the exclusiveness of the membership* — the more exclusive the membership the more those within the group will feel privileged and superior to outsiders;
- *external pressures* — where the group is under pressure, from whatever source, it is more likely to stick together;
- *similarities of members* — the more the members are alike in terms of their age, social background, education and so on, the more they are likely to identify with one another and share common attitudes;
- *commitment to group objectives* — the more the group feels that it has a valuable common purpose, the greater the degree of mutual commitment and support is likely to be;
- *the nature of the work* — if members of the group are undertaking similar work they are more likely to identify with each other;
- *ease of communication* — the easier it is for members of the group to communicate with each other, the more likely they are to do so and to reinforce their commitment to the group;
- *major rewards* — if by working together the group members can increase their potential rewards they are likely to seek greater co-operation;
- *group leadership* — an effective leader can increase group cohesiveness by encouraging members to work together.

Dangers of group think

Highly cohesive groups can be subject to the following dangers:

1. *An illusion of invulnerability* can result if group members feel a high degree of confident security and it can give them a distorted perception of their own infallibility. This means that they are more likely to take high risks.
2. *Shared stereotypes* can result in a total disregard for the strengths of outside groups, characterised by such statements as 'we know they are all useless'.
3. *Rationalisation* entails giving rational reasons for what are often feelings rather than conclusions based on a logical assessment of the facts.
4. *An illusion of morality* occurs when members of the group experience a feeling of superiority and excellence, leading to a belief that the group can do no wrong.
5. *Self censorship* occurs in such highly cohesive groups since people who have doubts may suppress them for fear of not being seen to support group objectives or of possibly damaging group harmony.
6. *Direct pressure* or even ridicule may be brought to bear if someone does venture an idea or opinion which runs counter to the group's general views. This in turn might lead others within the group to try to restore harmony in some way, possibly by diluting the point made by the offending party.
7. *An illusion of unanimity* may exist in such groups where silence may be perceived as consent and decisions are made without any real discussion.
8. *'Mind guard'* can be practised, where self-appointed guardians of the group's norms filter out any unwanted information or restrict the membership only to those who are likely to be in agreement with the general group view.

INTER-GROUP COMPETITION

Groups can be very effective mechanisms for getting things done in an organisation and they will form in any case whether or not that is the intention. While groups work in harmony, this is very much to the organisation's advantage. However, it can become a problem when groups become so committed to their own goals that they actively compete with other groups in a way that undermines the attainment of corporate objectives.

What happens in such situations is that each group becomes more closely knit and submerges internal differences. The climate of the group becomes less informal and more related to the task, while leadership tends to become more autocratic and the group more tolerant of such an approach, becoming more structured and organised. There is a greater demand for loyalty to present a united front, and each group tends to distort its perceptions, particularly seeing only its own strengths and the other group's weakness. Hostility between the groups and the negative stereotypes increase, and each group sees the other as an enemy. Finally, each group tends to listen only to arguments that support its own position.

GROUP EFFECTIVENESS

The effectiveness of any particular group depends on a number of factors (see Figure 7.1). Handy[3] describes these as:

- *the givens* — group, task and environment;
- *the intervening factors* — leadership style, processes and procedures, motivation;
- *the outcomes* — productivity, member satisfaction.

These factors are further broken down as follows.

Size

The larger the group the greater the diversity of talent, skills and knowledge, but the less chance there is of individual participation. Larger groups, ie with 20 members or more, are said to have more absenteeism and lower morale.

Member characteristics

The greater the similarity between people's attitudes, values and beliefs, the greater the degree of consensus.

Individual objectives and roles

The group is likely to be more effective if all its members have the same objectives. The problem is that most people have hidden agendas which can include:

- protecting the interests of a subgroup;
- scoring off an opponent;
- making a particular alliance;
- covering up;
- impressing others.

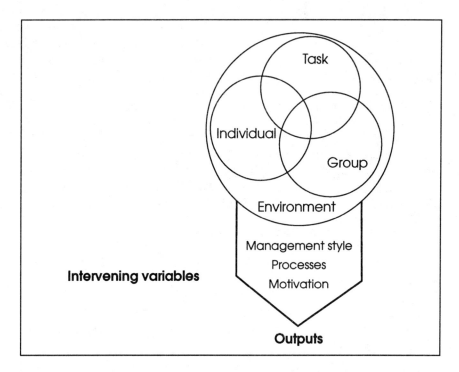

Figure 7.1 *Factors affecting group output*

It is therefore important for groups to establish common objectives and engender a level of mutual trust. The group can never hope to satisfy everybody's personal aims and ambitions.

Measures of team effectiveness

Measures of the effectiveness (or ineffectiveness) of a team include:

- attainment of targets;
- output;
- staff turnover;
- absence levels;
- complaints from customers/other departments;
- industrial action;
- grievances and disciplinary actions;
- poor timekeeping;
- accidents at work;
- accuracy and quality of work;
- staff motivation and morale (possibly as measured by all the above).

Stage of development

The effectiveness of the group depends on the stage it is at in the growth process described above — forming, storming, norming or performing.

The nature of the task

The kind of group will be determined by the kind of task undertaken. When the aim is problem solving, for example, a smaller group is more appropriate than when the role is information dissemination. Handy stresses that there should be one group for one role, otherwise there can be problems of ambiguity.

Criteria for effectiveness

The approach of the group will vary according to its timescale and the accuracy of the results required. The performance criteria will affect the way the group operates. If the task is urgent and straightforward a more autocratic approach might be required, whereas if it is longer term and complex much more discussion will be involved.

Salience of the task

The more important the task is to someone, the more likely that person is to be committed to the end results.

Clarity of the task

The clearer the task the more structured the group can be. On the other hand, the greater the ambiguity the more stress that is likely to be experienced by the group.

Norms and expectations

The culture, climate and working methods of the organisation will affect the way the group works, even though they may not be those most appropriate for the task in hand.

Leader position

The more powerful and respected the leader the greater his or her effect on group morale. If the group members feel that the leader is incapable of 'selling' or putting into effect their decisions, they are less likely to be committed to the tasks undertaken.

Leadership style

Clearly the way the leader behaves will affect group performance. Ideally the leader will be capable of adapting his or her management style to the needs of the situation, the task and the work group.

Inter-group relations

The extent to which the group is perceived as important and relevant to the overall goals of the organisation will affect the attitude of group members. There is likely to be less loyalty to a group which is felt to have no real standing within the organisation. If people no longer wish to contribute to group membership they will usually try either 'fight' or 'flight'. If they choose fight they will harness the negative aspects within the group so that it will attract more notice, albeit in a negative way. If they prefer flight, then they are likely to stop attending or contributing.

Physical location

As stated above, where there is close physical proximity there is increased interaction and greater co-operation. The physical location and even the way the workplace is organised can affect how groups are formed and their attitudes.

Processes and procedures

There are a number of processes or functions that have to be carried out by one or more people in the group at various times. These have been described as task and maintenance functions and are likely to include the following:

Task	Maintenance
Initiating	Encouraging
Information seeking	Compromising
Diagnosing	Peace keeping
Opinion seeking	Clarifying and summarising
Evaluating	Standard setting
Decision managing	

In any problem-solving group all the task functions listed should be carried out in the order suggested. The maintenance tasks are more about ensuring that the group continues to perform effectively.

Interaction pattern

The interaction pattern is the way in which the group members communicate with each other, and is usually described as either the wheel, the circle, the chain or the all-channel.[4] These are illustrated in Figure 7.2. Of the communication patterns:

- the wheel is quickest to reach a conclusion and the circle slowest;
- the all-channel approach is likely to give the best solution where the problem is complex;
- the level of satisfaction is lowest for individuals in the circle, fairly high in the all-channel, and mixed in the wheel.
- the chain is most appropriate when a task has to be accomplished quickly and there is little need for interaction among group members.

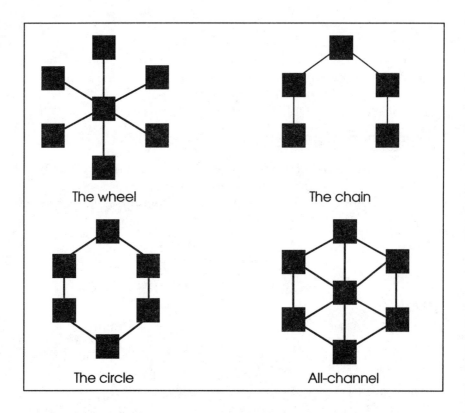

Figure 7.2   *Group interaction patterns*

Motivation

To be appropriately motivated an individual needs to be satisfied by membership of the group, to know the expected results or standards required, and to feel that the task is a valuable one.

CHARACTERISTICS OF AN EFFECTIVE GROUP

A group is effective when:

- all members of the group understand and accept the group's objectives;
- the working atmosphere is as relaxed and informal as circumstances permit;
- all members of the group are involved and contribute to discussion and there is a free exchange of views and personal feelings;
- no one particular person within the group dominates, but the leadership role changes as the occasion demands;
- disagreements are discussed and resolved with decisions being reached by a general consensus;
- there is an understanding of the decisions reached, follow-up action to be taken and results and timescales expected;
- the group is prepared to review its performance critically and to seek to improve that performance following completion of any particular task or project.

It is questionable whether groups do in fact make better decisions than individuals. Although the evidence suggests that groups are better at evaluating all options, there is the possibility that they will either reach an unsatisfactory compromise or take a higher risk decision. Studies broadly support the view that groups tend to take higher risks.

SPECIFIC GROUP TECHNIQUES

Brainstorming

Brainstorming is a way of generating a large number of ideas as quickly as possible. The box below illustrates how to carry out brainstorming. The basic principles are that:

- the emphasis is on the number of ideas generated rather than their quality;

- initially all ideas are accepted and none rejected;
- to start with there is no discussion or evaluation of ideas proposed;
- group members are invited to build on or elaborate ideas put forward.

There is no conclusive evidence that brainstorming is more effective than individual thinking.

How to brainstorm

1. Each person gives one idea.
2. Only one idea per turn.
3. Pass if no idea.
4. Do not discuss — at this stage.
5. Accept all ideas, however foolish.
6. Encourage exaggeration.
7. Do not criticise or ridicule.
8. Discuss and build on ideas.

Group dynamics and T-groups

Group dynamics is the study of interactions in small, face-to-face groups. One particular method is the 'T-group',[5] the 'T' standing for training. This normally comprises a small group of people who are unknown to each other. The group is totally unstructured with no leaders and no agenda or planned activities. The trainers who are present are there only as group facilitators, and take little active part in the proceedings.

The idea behind such a group is that the lack of structure and direction will cause anxiety and lead the group members to behave in ways which will increase their insight into their own patterns of behaviour. Such groups are dangerous tools, and there is no conclusive evidence that they increase personal effectiveness in the workplace. Whatever their advantages or disadvantages, such methods should never be used with work groups where people know each other well. To do so could damage working relationships irreparably.

These group activities — and there are many variants — are all designed to help people gain a better insight into themselves and others' perception of them. One particular tool that can help in reaching this understanding is the Johari window (see Figure 7.3).

	Known to self	Not known to self
Known to others	Public	Blind
Not known to others	Hidden	Unknown

Source: Luft[6]

Figure 7.3   *The Johari window*

The Public area comprises information known to the individual and to others, in other words the individual's public persona. The Hidden area is the part of the individual he or she chooses not to reveal, primarily attitudes and feelings. The Blind area refers to those attributes the individual has which are noticed by others but not recognised by the individual. The Unknown area comprises aspects of the individual's personality which are not known to that individual or to others, but which will affect his or her behaviour. Many group activities are designed to reach this hidden area.

AUTHORITY AND POWER

A group leader must have the authority to control the group. This can involve:

- allocating tasks to group members;
- giving rewards and imposing sanctions;
- communicating decisions by senior managers;
- representing the group within the organisation;
- taking decisions on behalf of the group;
- resolving conflicts and difficulties within the group.

However, authority is not the same as power, which can be exercised by any member of the group. Indeed a powerful group member can supplant the official group leader as the informal leader.

French and Raven[7] identified the following sources of power in an organisation:

1. *Reward power* — which is based on the perception that a particular person is able to give rewards, whether in the form of pay, promotion, recognition or privileges.

particular person is able to give rewards, whether in the form of pay, promotion, recognition or privileges.

2. *Coercive power* — based on the perception that an individual can punish a group member, possibly by withholding benefits or privileges, but equally by generating fear in some other way.

3. *Legitimate power* — based on the individual's legitimate position within the organisation. Where, for example, someone is appointed to the post of supervisor, he or she is given the power associated with that position in the organisation.

4. *Referent power* — derives from an individual's identification with a particular person because of his or her personal characteristics. This is sometimes referred to as charisma.

5. *Expert power* — derives from the perception that an individual is an expert in a particular area and that advice within the area of expertise will therefore be respected.

6. *Information power* — is power that an individual derives because he or she is the only one with access to information required by other people.

Finally, there is another source of power which French and Raven do not mention:

7. *Derived power* — when an individual gains power not from the position occupied but rather from that occupied by someone on whose behalf he or she can act. For example, the managing director's secretary, or someone appointed to carry out a special project for the chairman, is likely to have a considerable amount of influence within the organisation.

The point about these sources of power in an organisation is that they may not necessarily be established in a particular leader, but could be spread among different members of a group. They do, of course, overlap and one particular individual might have more than one source of power. In general terms the more sources of power an individual has, the greater his or her influence within the group is likely to be.

WHAT IS THE IDEAL TEAM?

When trying to form a work team, particularly at management level, it is a tantalising thought that what is really required is a mixture of abilities. You need someone to produce ideas, someone else to put those ideas into action, another person to ensure that everybody makes a contribution and that as many ideas as possible are considered, someone to evaluate critically any suggestions and bring the others down to earth, and so on.

The problem is that organisations rarely start with a blank sheet of paper and have to make do with the people they have already got, especially as team membership very often depends on the position occupied rather than the individual personality. It is very likely that any group of people will have an unequal distribution of characteristics. These may not be the characteristics required or give the right balance to the team.

There is also the question of what roles might be appropriate for any particular team. It may well be that what is considered desirable is not necessarily the best combination. However, notwithstanding these objections, it probably does make good sense to try to have a variety of skills and approaches in a team, depending on what its role is. Certainly it is as well to have the enthusiastic ideas person counterbalanced by someone who may be somewhat more cautious and who will see the costs as well as the benefits of any course of action.

Through research Belbin[8] identified eight different types of contribution from group members. These are described below.

One person may be performing more than one role at the same time, but teams are likely to work most effectively if there is a combination of individuals in roles, as appropriate to the demands of the task, each carried out by a person suited to that particular role.

Chairman

The chairman's role is to direct the group, but this is done without being too assertive. He or she will guide and coordinate the discussion and might intervene at critical points, but will do so without offending people. The chairman tends to be goal orientated and knows how to make the best use of team resources.

Shaper

The shaper's main concern is to attain the goals of the group, by whatever means necessary. The shaper is likely to be highly motivated with a high need for achievement and to display a great deal of nervous energy. He or she will be suspicious and impatient and will be likely to react aggressively to challenges and show emotion following any form of disappointment or frustration. Shapers are excellent at generating action but would have a limited usefulness in a team which was already working well.

Plant

The plant is the person who produces the ideas in the group. He or she is likely to be very intelligent and often has radical ideas, with little regard for practical constraints. The plant tends to think independently and not be very team orientated. Plants also tend to be introverts and may need to be brought out by other members of the group. Handled well and given praise and support, a plant can greatly benefit the group, but such people can just as easily lose interest and play no useful part in the team.

Monitor evaluator

The monitor evaluator is the one who evaluates the quality of ideas in the group. This person may appear to be somewhat indifferent to the team and for the most part play no active role except when a crucial decision is about to be made.

The monitor evaluator is very good at weighing all the facts and options available and coming to a well-considered view which is likely to be objective and unemotional. This can be a useful role in a team, although people who perform it may be perceived as somewhat dry and overcritical. While this person may not be very motivated in terms of the group, he or she is likely to stop it from moving in the wrong direction.

Company worker

Company workers are the implementers and organisers of the group. They prefer orderliness and routine and are concerned with detail. The company worker identifies with the organisation and has a capacity for hard work. Because of this he or she may be left to deal with the more difficult or undesirable tasks.

Resource investigator

The resource investigator is very good at picking up ideas and making them work. This person is very adept at finding out what is available and what can be done and will be sociable, friendly and generally extrovert. Although this role is valuable for putting ideas into practice, enthusiasm for specific issues may be short lived.

Team worker

The team worker is a good communicator who places the group's objectives and maintaining the team before his or her own individual ambitions. While the person occupying this role will be perceptive and diplomatic, he or she will not be one of the decision makers in the group. The main function of the role is to dampen conflict and smooth out difficulties.

Finisher

The finisher is someone who is very good at tying up the loose ends. This is a person who pays attention to detail and organises work to ensure that results are achieved. The finisher is likely to be tenacious and unwilling to let things go unfinished, but can have a tendency to get bogged down in detail when projects may no longer be worth pursuing. He or she will, however, help to ensure that the group meets deadlines and gets things done.

EMPOWERED TEAMS

'Empowerment' is a term which is currently in vogue. It really means delegating accountabilities and decision making to the lowest competent level in the organisation so that decisions can be made closest to their point of impact. This should be a characteristic of any organisation which seeks to make the best possible use of its human resources.

Making decisions as close as possible to their point of impact has the advantage that they are likely to be better decisions, because the people concerned are likely to be those who are best informed about the relevant issues, and that the delegation of responsibility in this way is usually more likely to increase motivation and morale. In effect, the organisation is communicating its strategy and values to team members so that they know what has to be achieved, but the means of achieving the required results is left to the people concerned. For this to work effectively, the employees must wholeheartedly embrace the organisation's values and be committed to the organisation's overall direction. They must also know that by taking calculated risks which may go beyond the limits of their existing job they will receive the appropriate rewards, provided their actions support the overall strategic direction.

The characteristics of an empowered organisation can be summarised as:

1. *An assumption of competence* — which means that there is a belief that people can be trusted to get on with their work and there is therefore a minimal need for checks, controls, directives and layers of supervision and management.
2. *Curiosity* — in learning from others and about how the company operates.
3. *Forgiveness* — so that some mistakes are tolerated. This may be contrasted with what typically happens in organisations. It

is probably a rule that those who thrive are the ones who are not seen to make serious errors. The problem with this is that it rewards those who avoid taking risks and overlooks the fact that the real 'doers' in organisations are the ones who may be prepared to stick their necks out sometimes. On the other hand, of course, all risks should be calculated ones and organisations cannot afford to keep people who frequently make major mistakes. The trick is to get the balance right.

4.   *Trust* — empowerment requires a situation of high trust and high competence. There is little point in employing highly competent people if they are not given a high degree of trust and at the same time people need to be highly competent if they are to be given this trust.

5.   *Togetherness* — this means working in flexible teams regardless of members' status or position in the hierarchy, and operating with shared goals and values.

The advantages of empowerment

The advantages of empowerment are that:

● flexible teams are more likely to be able to respond quickly to market and organisational demands;
● the requirement for fewer checks, controls and layers of management will reduce overhead costs;
● it is likely to make use of creative potential throughout the organisation;
● empowered teams are more likely to have high motivation and morale because of the opportunities for growth and development provided by such a culture;
● empowerment also implies working in multi-disciplinary teams across the organisation and this will help to break down barriers between functions and improve understanding;
● there will be increased responsiveness to customer demands as issues will be more easily dealt with by the part of the organisation which is in contact with the customer.

Building empowered teams

Building an empowered organisation will need to include the following stages:

1.   Top level commitment to the concept of empowerment and clarity about the organisation's values and strategy.

2. Development of a plan for achieving empowerment, accepting that this may be quite a long process.

3. A review of the organisation's structure and processes to consider how these can be improved and streamlined, and particularly how empowered multi-functional teams can cut across departmental and functional boundaries to produce results in critical processes.

4. A review of human resources policies and reward processes to determine the company's reward strategy, particularly in relation to team performance.

5. Communication of the concept and approach and the organisation's overall strategy and values to all employees.

6. Training and further employment of employees as required.

References

[1] Tuckman, B W (1965) 'Development sequence in small groups', *Psychological Bulletin*, 63.

[2] Janis, I L (1972) *Victims of Group Think*, Houghton-Mifflin, Boston.

[3] Handy, C B (1985) *Understanding Organizations*, 3rd edn, Penguin, Harmondsworth.

[4] See Bavelas, A and Barrett, D (1951) 'An experimental approach to organizational communication', *Personnel*, 27; and Leavitt, H J (1951) 'Some effects of certain communication patterns on group performance', *Journal of Abnormal and Social Psychology*, 46.

[5] Blumberg, A T and Golembiewski, R T (1976) *Learning and Change in Groups*, Penguin, Harmondsworth.

[6] Luft, J (1984) *Group Processes: An Introduction to Group Dynamics*, 3rd edn, Mayfield Publishing, California.

[7] French, J R P and Raven, B (1968) 'The bases of social power' in Cartwright, D and Zander, A F *Group Dynamics: Research and Theory*, 3rd edn, Harper and Row, New York.

[8] Belbin, R M (1981) *Management Teams: Why they succeed or fail*, Heinemann, Oxford.

Motivation and Reward

WHAT IS MOTIVATION AND WHY IS IT IMPORTANT?

Motivation describes why people behave in a particular way to achieve a set of objectives. In the work context, motivation theory specifically seeks to answer such questions as:

- What will make employees work harder?
- How can employee performance be improved?
- How can attendance at work be improved?
- What sorts of pay and performance bonuses will be most effective?
- What working arrangements will produce the best levels of performance?

The questions above, and many others like them, are typical of those that managers will ask themselves when trying to decide how to get the best possible performance from their staff. The key to any organisations's success is the performance of its employees and it is generally accepted that the quality of this performance will depend on the employees' attitudes to their employer.

Any employee has a contract of employment which states or implies that he or she should use the best endeavours to carry out particular duties and responsibilities, in return for which the employer will give a certain level of reward, normally comprising pay and benefits. The content of such an employment contract is usually clear to both parties. However, there is in addition something which could be described as a psychological contract. This comprises the unwritten expectations of the individual and the organisation. For example, the individual will expect the organisation to provide a reasonably safe and healthy working environment and to treat people fairly. In return, the organisation will expect a fair day's work for a fair day's pay, loyalty and so on.

What is important from the organisation's viewpoint is to try to ensure that an individual's reasonable expectations are met. If they are not, the individual may become alienated and will not work to the best of his or her ability.

Motivation theory attempts to define what makes people perform well. This should help employers to focus on those factors that would be likely to make the most difference, but unfortunately there is no real consensus about this. The main theories are summarised below.

THEORIES OF MOTIVATION

Broadly speaking, theories of motivation fall into two categories: content theories that focus on people's needs and goals, and process theories that are concerned more with how people behave and why they behave in a particular way. The most important of both these are described below.

F W Taylor and scientific management

F W Taylor[1] was one of the leading exponents of 'scientific management'. This approach concentrates on making work as efficient as possible by streamlined work methods, division of labour and work measurement. Jobs are broken into their various components, measured using work study techniques and rewarded according to productivity. Under this approach, motivation comes from the financial incentives achievable through meeting output targets. It is this thinking that is behind most work study based incentive schemes.

The major problem with this approach is that it works on the assumption that money is a key motivator. However, the extent to which this is true will vary from person to person and job to job. People who are working on a production line or carrying out unpleasant and difficult manual tasks are unlikely to be motivated by the work itself. In such circumstances money is likely to be a prime motivator and greater effort will be made only if it will lead to increased earnings.

On the other hand, where jobs are of a more professional or managerial nature, the rewards are likely to be more diverse and the payment of bonuses may not, of itself, produce commensurate increases in productivity or efficiency.

The other point that needs to be borne in mind is that money itself is only a means to an end. It is only valuable because it will result in an improved quality of life or enhanced status within and outside the organisation.

It is likely that Taylor's scientific management approach is partly true. Certainly the right level of incentive payments for people undertaking production based jobs is likely to lead to increased productivity and more effort. However, care needs to be exercised to ensure that there is no deterioration in quality.

Furthermore, while money may be an incentive for certain categories of people it is unlikely to have the same impact for people whose jobs are not output based. There may be difficulties in measuring outputs in many cases, and money is more likely to provide a short-term incentive rather than gain long-term commitment.

Maslow's hierarchy of needs

Whenever individual motivation is discussed, Maslow's hierarchy of needs is inevitably mentioned[2] (see Figure 8.1). This is based on the assumption that once people have satisfied a certain level of need, they will want to move to the level above. Maslow described five levels of need, as follows:

- *physiological needs* — those that have to be satisfied to stay alive, including food, shelter, clothing, air to breathe and so on.
- *safety needs* — once a person's basic physiological needs are satisfied, attention can then be turned to satisfying safety needs. These include being safe from any kind of physical threat or deprivation and feeling secure. Once someone has sufficient income to be able to meet all physiological needs, for example to buy food and housing, then attention will be turned to providing security though insurance policies, trade union subscriptions and so on.
- *love or social needs* — once a person has satisfied physiological and safety needs, the next concern is likely to be with relationships. The love and affection required at this level may be realised through deep interpersonal relationships but will also be reflected in the need to belong to various social groups. In the work context, therefore, while people may carry out a particular job because of the need to earn money to maintain their basic lifestyle, they also value work because of the social relationships it generates.
- *esteem needs* — self-confidence and self-respect as well as the need for recognition by others. In the work context, this means

having a job which a person can recognise as valuable, providing a sense of achievement and general recognition and prestige in the outside world.

- *self-actualisation needs* — this is at the top of Maslow's hierarchy and refers to the desire for self-fulfilment. Provided all the other needs have been satisfied a person is likely to want to achieve his or her full potential. This final stage will probably be attained by relatively few people.

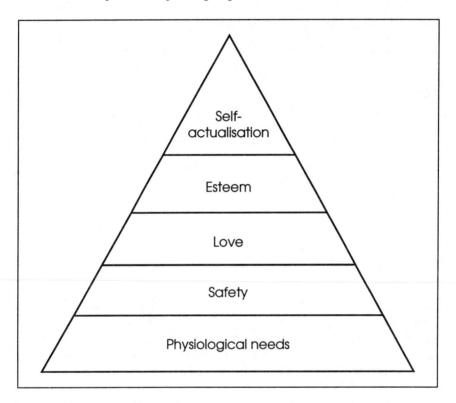

Figure 8.1   *Maslow's hierarchy of needs*

While Maslow's hierarchy of needs is much quoted and does make intuitive sense, it is probably of limited value in helping managers to motivate staff. This is because:

- aspects of the hierarchy will vary in importance between individuals — not everyone is seeking self-actualisation and some people may be quite content with a job which provides a good standard of living and relative security but few opportunities for individual development;

- some aspects of employment may satisfy a number of different needs at the same time;
- to apply the theory in an organisation would mean that managers would have to be clear about where a person was on the hierarchy, and even then it would be unlikely that there would be sufficient flexibility within the organisation to be able to produce rewards appropriate to that person's needs;
- there is an implied assumption that satisfying the needs mentioned would result in increased motivation and performance, but this is not necessarily the case.

In general, therefore, while Maslow's theory is a useful framework it does not greatly help managers in devising policies to motivate staff.

Alderfer's ERG theory

Alderfer[3] redefined Maslow's hierarchy into three groups, described as existence, relatedness and growth (ERG):

- *Existence needs* are all those relating to sustaining human existence and correspond to the physiological and security needs of the Maslow hierarchy.
- *Relatedness needs* concern social and personal relationships.
- *growth needs* are those concerned with the development of individual potential and relate to Maslow's esteem and self-actualisation needs.

According to ERG theory all of these needs can exist at the same time. If one particular level of need cannot be satisfied, then a person is likely to turn to another level. For example, if that person's job does not provide opportunities for self-development, then he or she might instead concentrate on social relations, that is relatedness rather than growth. The implication for managers is that if a particular job does not, for example, give opportunities for self-development then consideration should be given to other aspects of the job, such as enhanced pay and benefits or social activities.

Herzberg's motivation-hygiene theory

Based on research interviews with US accountants and engineers from different industries, Herzberg developed a two-factor theory of motivation.[4] This postulated that there are some factors which, if absent, cause dissatisfaction and which are separate from other motivating factors which encourage superior effort and performance. The former, dissatisfiers, he described as hygiene factors and the latter, satisfiers, he described as motivators (see table opposite).

Hygiene factors	Motivators
Company policy and administration	Achievement
Supervision	Recognition
Salary	Nature of the work
Interpersonal relations	Responsibility
Working conditions	Advancement

Herzberg's theory is that the hygiene factors will not motivate staff, but if they are considered to be unsatisfactory in some way, for example because salaries are not high enough or working conditions are unpleasant, they can be strong sources of potential dissatisfaction. The motivators, on the other, hand, are those factors which are likely to encourage higher performance and better quality work. The prospect for advancement, for example, might make someone work harder although at the same time the lack of any such prospect may not be sufficient to make that person leave.

One interesting aspect of Herzberg's theory is that pay is not considered to be a motivator. In many cases, particularly for professional and managerial staff, this may well be true. Provided that salaries received are adequate and perceived by the people concerned to be fair in relation to their peers, then the annual salary increase may not be enough to induce superior performance. On the other hand, recognition, advancement and opportunities for self-development may well provide such an incentive.

Of course, not everybody thinks this way. Blue-collar jobs are frequently undertaken by people who are not doing the work because of any intrinsic value they derive from it, but because it pays the bills. This has been described as an 'instrumental' attitude to work and was found to be a common approach among assembly line car workers in Luton.[5] Such jobs can be tedious, and rewarding only through the pay rates offered.

Whether or not money is a motivator remains an open question. Probably the truth is that it motivates certain people at certain times. However, in many other cases it is not the money that will make people perform better but the other motivating factors identified by Herzberg. It is also worth bearing in mind that some people may confuse money with recognition. In other words, if people feel that they are not paid well enough in relation to their peers, or because of the amount of effort they put in, they might ask for more money to achieve recognition and fair treatment, which might be what is really motivating them.

One other criticism of Herzberg's approach is that his research methodology could have encouraged the employees concerned to state that money was not a motivator whereas in reality it was.

McGregor's theory X and theory Y

McGregor's theory X and theory Y[6] are discussed in more detail in Chapter 9. However, it is necessary to note here that, according to McGregor, theory X managers regard workers as inherently lazy and are therefore inclined to use a 'carrot and stick' approach to management, whereas theory Y managers take the view that work is as natural as rest and play, and that people are basically inclined to work hard and do a good job. The theory that a manager espouses will obviously affect the way he or she manages and motivates staff.

The theory of complex man

The problem with most of the motivation theories mentioned above is that they all assume that people are motivated by a particular kind of drive. The underlying models may be described as:

- *economic man* — who is motivated primarily by financial rewards;
- *social man* — whose motivation is affected primarily by the nature of relationships at work, derived mainly from the work of Elton Mayo[7] and the 'Hawthorne' experiments. These were a series of studies conducted at Western Electric's Hawthorne Works in the 1920s and 1930s. The most interesting aspect of these studies was that when the lighting and other working conditions were improved for one particular work group, but kept the same for another, the productivity of both groups improved, contrary to expectations. Furthermore, when, in further experiments, the conditions were worsened, productivity still continued to improve.

  The reason for this, apparently, was because of the interest shown in the people in the groups. Being at the centre of attention improved morale and productivity.

  This phenomenon came to be known as 'The Hawthorne Effect' and gave rise to the human relations movement, where the emphasis on improving productivity moved away from the classical and scientific management approaches, to focus instead on the management of human relationships.
- *self-actualising man* — as suggested by Maslow's hierarchy of needs and McGregor's theory Y.

In reality all these models are oversimplifications as people are all different and will have different motivations, which will in any case change over time. This more complex model Schein[8] has described as complex man. The implication of this is that managers are unlikely to be able to find one particular approach that motivates everybody and should therefore adopt a managerial style that is flexible according to the circumstances. This is considered in more detail in Chapter 9.

Achievement motivation theory

McClelland[9] stressed the importance of the need for achievement, as the achievers in business and industry are the ones who get things done. He identified three main motivations:

- affiliation;
- power;
- achievement.

Unlike Maslow, however, McClelland did not see these motivations in a hierarchy, but rather varying between individuals and occupations. He identified the following common characteristics of people with high achievement needs:

- a liking for situations in which a person can assume personal responsibility;
- a tendency to set moderate goals and take calculated risks;
- a desire for unambiguous feedback on performance.

What this implies for the management and development of managers is that achievement motivation can be developed. People learn faster and better when they are highly motivated to achieve a task, and because they are highly motivated to achieve their goals, achievers welcome advice and suggestions on how they can improve their performance.

Expectancy theory

Expectancy theory is based on the belief that people will be influenced by their perception of the likely results of their actions. For example, people who want promotion will perform well if they consider that high performance will be recognised and rewarded by promotion.

Vroom[10] developed a theory based on what he described as valence, instrumentality and expectancy. Valence is a person's preference for a particular outcome. This outcome might, for example, be high productivity. However, this is likely to be valued only to the extent that it might help the person achieve other outcomes, such as a salary increase or promotion. The extent to which these second-level outcomes may be achieved is defined as instrumentality. Finally, expectancy refers to the strength of the person's belief that certain activities will lead to a certain result.

The implications of this for managers are that the link between reward and effort should be made very clear and that rewards, as far as possible, should meet individual employees' needs. The problem, of course, is that every person's needs and expectations are different and while some people may be motivated by financial rewards, others will be more interested in promotion and self-development.

Vroom's theory was further developed by Porter and Lawler.[11] They indicated that increased effort does not necessarily lead to higher performance as there are a number of other variables to be taken into account. These include:

- the person's perception of the value of the reward;
- the extent to which people expect a certain result from a particular course of action;
- the amount of effort put in by people;
- particular abilities, traits and skills which affect how well a person carries out the job;
- how people view their role within the organisation and what they consider to be appropriate behaviour;
- perceptions of what is a fair reward for the effort expended;
- the person's satisfaction with the job and the organisation.

All the factors listed by Porter and Lawler are overlapping and interdependent. While it is highly likely that they will all affect someone's motivation, it is difficult to establish clear cause and effect. For example, while job satisfaction is likely to lead to higher performance, it is also true that high performance is likely to lead to high job satisfaction.

The Porter and Lawler model does help to illustrate that motivating staff and gaining higher performance are far from straightforward and will be influenced by a number of variables. All that managers can hope to do is to be aware of all these variations and take them into account when designing work systems and considering rewards.

Other theories

There are a number of other theories about motivation at work, including the following:

1. *Equity theory* — this highlights the fact that a person's motivation is likely to be affected by the perception of how

favourably he or she has been treated within the organisation when compared with others. If people feel that their treatment is less favourable than that of those whom they compare themselves with, it is likely that they will be less motivated to perform well.

2. *Goal theory* — this is based on the belief that people's goals will determine how they behave at work and the amount of effort they put in. There are indications that having clear goals does help to motivate people, and this would tend to suggest that organisations should seek to develop comprehensive performance management schemes.

3. *Attribution theory* — this postulates that motivation will be dependent on internal factors such as a person's personal attributes, and external factors which might be the organisation's policies, the degree of difficulty of the work undertaken and so on.

SUMMARY

There are a whole range of theories and beliefs about what motivates people in organisations. In regard to almost all the theories proposed there is evidence both for and against. On the whole there is no consensus about motivation and it is therefore very difficult for organisations to be prescriptive and to arrive at policies and approaches that will satisfy everybody. It is also impractical in an organisation of any size to carry out an in-depth analysis of what motivates any one person. There are, however, certain practical rules which can be followed to at least help motivate staff and improve job satisfaction. These are:

1. Make it clear to employees what is meant by effective performance and ensure that they know what is expected of them.

2. Ensure that there is, as far as possible, a clear link between performance and rewards and that any such link is clearly communicated to employees.

3. Ensure that all staff are treated fairly and that judgements about performance are objective.

4. Where possible, develop different kinds of reward — not everyone can be promoted or would necessarily want to be.

5. Encourage as much flexibility as possible in the working environment and develop management styles that are adaptive and capable of being changed to suit the person and the circumstances.

6. Develop a comprehensive system of performance management or, at least, set people targets that are attainable but stretching.

7. Take account of all relevant environmental and social factors, such as the comfort and facilities of the working environment, social interactions among people, heating or lighting — that is, all those factors that could be potential sources of dissatisfaction.

IMPLICATIONS FOR REWARD MANAGEMENT

When deciding how to pay people in an organisation the following considerations should apply.

Money as a motivator

Money may not actually motivate people. Surprisingly, there is no clear evidence that increased earnings will necessarily lead to higher performance. However, there are likely to be big differences in the attitudes towards earnings of different industry sectors and employee groups. For example, people who are carrying out routine manual or production line jobs that provide little intrinsic job satisfaction may well be motivated to increase output (though not necessarily quality) for more pay.

It is also probably true that if salary levels are not considered adequate by people in the organisation, this will be a source of dissatisfaction. For this reason organisations should have regard to market rates, although the extent to which they are obliged to pay them will depend on the current economic climate. In a recession, employees are more reluctant to change jobs and employers' recruitment and retention problems are likely to be minimal. Although it is possible to pay less than the market rate in such a climate, there could be costs in terms of individual motivation and future retention.

Performance-related pay

Although performance-related pay appears to be an attractive proposition, it is very difficult to implement effectively. The organisation has to be confident that it can measure performance accurately and introduce a scheme that is objective and perceived to be fair. This means that there must first be a comprehensive system of performance management that accurately identifies performance measures and different levels of performance. Any scheme which fails to do this is more likely to cause dissatisfaction and demotivate employees than motivate them.

A further problem of relating pay to performance occurs in setting appropriate targets. For example, there are many companies that have more than one division operating in different product areas, and it is not uncommon for some to benefit from a buoyant market at the same time as others are suffering a collapse in demand. In such circumstances there is a danger, if targets are not carefully set and reviewed, that those who attain their targets with relative ease gain large bonuses whereas others who may be working much harder fail to meet their targets and do not, as a consequence, receive any bonus. Clearly any scheme that operated in this way would be divisive and unfair.

Another problem of relating pay to performance is how to reward those jobs where it is difficult to set output targets. Examples include legal, administrative and research roles, where outputs are very difficult to measure. In such cases a competency based approach might be required, in which the organisation rewards successful behaviours rather than tangible outputs. This again can lead to difficulties over managing the process and ensuring that the system is both fair and perceived to be fair.

Finally, any target-setting process would need to include a mixture of short-term and long-term targets, otherwise there could be a focus on immediate results to the detriment of the organisation's long-term future. There could be difficulty in establishing and rewarding such long-term targets.

Long-term rewards

While some kind of payment related to performance is one means of rewarding people, it is more appropriate for use in the relatively short term. The organisation should also have systems for rewarding employees over the long term as they build up experience and expertise within the organisation. Salary levels should be perceived as being fair in relation to what other people are receiving. If people feel that they are receiving less money, or are being paid at a lower grade, than someone who is undertaking a similar level of work, they are likely to be demotivated. Therefore there is also probably a need for some analytical means of determining job size to ensure that people are paid equitably.

Bonus schemes

There are, of course, many different types of bonus incentive scheme operating in manual and craft jobs. These kinds of jobs lend themselves to this approach because there are clear outputs and work is, therefore, easily measured. Such work study based incentive schemes have been in existence for many years, since the days of scientific management, and no doubt do produce the desired results where cash bonuses are a key motivating factor and unit output is a prime performance measure. There are, however, a number of problems with such schemes as they can:

- discourage a team approach if incentives are individually based;
- encourage a short-term focus on immediate outputs rather than long-term improvements and development;
- lead to manipulation and control of work outputs and methods by certain employees;
- fail to produce the projected productivity savings while costing money to implement and maintain;
- be divisive.

Management incentives that failed

In one particular FMCG (fast moving consumer goods) company some divisions were badly hit by the recession whereas others were relatively recession proof. All managers were part of a bonus incentive scheme which rewarded the attainment of profit targets. The managers in the hardest-hit divisions were working round the clock but still making losses because of the difficult market, and therefore not receiving any bonuses. In contrast, the managers in the relatively favourable markets were not working particularly hard but still meeting their targets, and consequently being paid handsome bonuses.

The real problem here was the company's failure to adjust targets to take account of business realities, and as a consequence morale was lowered in the divisions which were not performing so well. The obvious unfairness of the bonus scheme resulted in the company abandoning it in favour of a completely subjective approach in which the chief executive allocated bonuses on the basis of his judgement about the managers' performance.

Conclusion

The conclusion to be drawn from the above is that no hard evidence exists that money alone will motivate employees, although it is highly likely that it will work for some people. On the other hand, if the rewards paid are not seen to be fair and equitable, or at the right level in relation to the external market, this is likely to be a source of real

What motivates you?

The following self-assessment questionnaire may help to illustrate the relative importance of different motivational factors.

Rank each item below in order of importance to you. Compare your results with your colleagues. What do they imply?

Pay

Good colleagues

Pleasant working environment

Promotion prospects

Good benefits

Holidays

Hours of work

Sense of achievement

Job challenge

Variety

Security

Recognition

Training

Status

Doing a worthwhile job

Interesting work

dissatisfaction. Whatever reward system is implemented, it should be based on sound research and objective measurement and, most importantly, be perceived as fair by the organisation's employees.

This conclusion can be tested by completing the questionnaire on the previous page. Complete it to find out what motivates you and your colleagues.

References

1   Taylor, F W (1947) 'The principles of scientific management' in *Scientific Management*, Harper and Row, New York.
2   Maslow, A H (1943) 'A theory of human motivation', *Psychological Review*, 50.
3   Alderfer, C P (1972) *Existence, Relatedness and Growth*, Collier Macmillan, New York.
4   Herzberg, F (1966) *Work and the Nature of Man*, World Publishing Co, New York.
5   Goldthorpe J, Lockwood, D, Bechofer, F and Platt, J (1968) *The Affluent Worker*, Cambridge University Press, Cambridge.
6   McGregor, D M (1960) *The Human Side of Enterprise*, McGraw-Hill, New York.
7   Roethlisberger, F J and Dickson, W J (1939) *Management and the Worker*, Harvard University Press, Harvard.
8   Schein, E H (1980) *Organizational Psychology*, 3rd edn, Prentice-Hall, New Jersey.
9   McClelland, D C (1961) *The Achieving Society*, Van Nostrand Reinhold, New Jersey.
10   Vroom, V H (1964) *Work and Motivation*, Wiley, New York.
11   Porter, L W and Lawler, E E (1968) *Managerial Attitudes and Performance*, Irwin, Homewood, Illinois.

The Management Role

This chapter is concerned with the role of the manager in an organisation. It explores what is meant by management, different styles of management, the kinds of issues managers should consider and approaches they should apply to carry out their role effectively.

MANAGEMENT AND LEADERSHIP

It could be argued that management and leadership are one and the same thing. However, it is probably important to distinguish between the two as not all managers are leaders and not all management jobs require leadership. There are, for example, a large number of jobs in organisations which might involve the planning and management of the organisation's direction and strategy, but which do not involve the post holder in directly leading staff. There are also a number of aspects of the management role that are quite distinct from leadership.

However, even though there is a clear distinction between the two, the emphasis in this chapter will be very much on the manager as a leader. Leadership is a key role of managers and it is in this area that the real differences in performance and productivity can be made.

Leadership refers to the process by which people are influenced in such a way that they attain the goals being attempted in a particular situation. Management has been described as getting the job done through people, and the manager's performance will depend on his or her ability as a leader.

There are a number of different definitions of management, but they usually include, to varying degrees, the following aspects:

1. *Planning* — the organisation's strategy and how it can be

achieved. This can include deciding the general direction to be followed and drawing up a plan accordingly.

2. *Organising* — once the organisation has its strategies and plans clearly defined (whether written down or not) the next step is to organise its resources and people to achieve the desired results.

3. *Controlling* — this entails ensuring that the organisation's activities are directed to the results required and making any adjustments where necessary, such as reallocating work or changing jobs. It includes coordinating different parts of the organisation to ensure that they are all pulling in the same direction.

4. *Motivating* — this means managing the organisation's staff so that they perform effectively.

5. *Communication* — this can be added to the other four functions, although it is not really a separate aspect of management but rather a skill that needs to underlie every aspect of the management role. The manager has to ensure that the organisation's messages are clear to employees, customers, subordinates, peers and superiors.

THE LEADERSHIP PROCESS

We have said above that a key role of management is leadership. This means being able to influence the members of a particular group to achieve the results required. It also means ensuring that the group will continue to give loyalty and support and work effectively for any future tasks they undertake.

In carrying out this role the leader has to ensure that full use is made of the group's strengths and qualities and that any weaknesses are tackled. The manager has to take account of four elements: the task, the group, the individual and the environment (see Figure 9.1).[1]

The nature of the task

Some tasks will be complex and will need to be carried out over a long period and use a range of skills. For example, the preparation of a corporate plan for an organisation will need to call on a number of different functions: finance, personnel, operations, marketing, sales and so on, and the coordination of these professional inputs is likely to be complex. Contrast this with a production line job involving a number of different but straightforward tasks at each stage and it is clear that a different approach will be required.

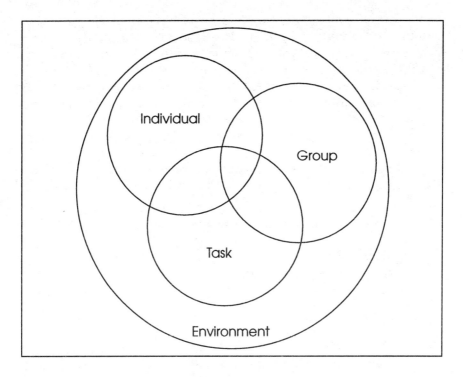

Figure 9.1 *Factors affecting management style*

The role of the manager is to:

- make clear what outputs are required;
- ensure that everybody understands his or her role;
- understand how any particular task fits into the overall organ-isation and its objectives;
- plan how the task should be carried out;
- determine what resources are required;
- allocate resources as appropriate;
- ensure that the processes and organisation structure are appropriate to the task;
- monitor the progress of the task;
- evaluate results and review the overall process.

The various roles of the manager as a leader are summarised on page 154.

The group

All groups are different and each has its own collective personality. The leader of the group must understand these different influences and also remember that he or she is at the same time part of the group and separate from it. The leader will at times need to represent the interests of the group but will also need to ensure that they fulfil the organisation's objectives. One of the classic problems in organisations is that of the first-line supervisor who has been promoted from the work group into the supervisory role. If this person identifies too closely with the group members, it may be difficult for him or her to take unpopular decisions and exercise firm control.

The role of the leader in relation to the group is to:

- set objectives for the group as a whole;
- ensure that the group functions cohesively as a unit;
- allocate work in the way that best uses the strengths of the group;
- represent the interests of the group;
- handle any conflicts arising;
- build a team or group identity.

The individual

The leader must remember that everyone within the group has his or her own motivations and expectations. Each person has to fit into the team and someone who does not is likely to work less effectively, and could have a disruptive effect on the team as a whole. This does not mean that all members of the team necessarily have to like each other, but they do have to cooperate so that the team's targets are met.

The role of the manager is to:

- ensure that each individual is clear about his or her role within the group;
- set individual targets and monitor performance against those targets;
- give people positive feedback about their performance;
- be aware, as far as possible, of individual difficulties and problems that might affect performance;
- ensure that members of the team receive all necessary training appropriate to the job they are carrying out;
- try to ensure that the work carried out by an individual gives him or her a sense of achievement and satisfaction;
- try to encourage the feeling in people that the work they are doing is advancing them or developing them in some way;
- give each person as much control as possible over his or her own work; in other words, delegate.

Probably the most challenging role of the leader is trying to reconcile the different and possibly conflicting demands of the objectives to be achieved by the organisation, the objectives of the work group, and the individual aims and aspirations of each member of that group. A match between all three is likely to lead to high performance and high job satisfaction.

The environment

It must be remembered that all of this takes place in the context of the environment. The way work is carried out and people's attitudes to managers and the organisation will be influenced by the climate and culture of the organisation. Membership of a small professional firm of lawyers will be very different from being in a large industrial conglomerate. Large factories and manufacturing plants are likely to have a very different atmosphere and group norms to those of a small, well-appointed office.

The general climate will also be affected by how well the organisation is doing. Organisations that are striving to survive with the threat of impending redundancies will have a very different atmosphere from those that are riding the crest of the wave. Some organisations will be old-fashioned and bureaucratic whereas others will be informal and use the latest technology. Timescales will also vary enormously. In a pharmaceutical research laboratory results may not be achieved for ten or more years. In a packaging plant, on the other hand, production targets will have to be met on a daily basis and might change dramatically during the week.

There is perhaps little that a manager can do to change the environment. The most important thing is that the manager is flexible enough to adapt to changes in that environment and to ensure that the group for which he or she is responsible does the same.

THEORIES OF LEADERSHIP

There have been a number of theories of leadership. Some of the earliest concentrated on highlighting the traits necessary for good leaders. It is still an unanswered question whether good leaders are born or can be made. Very likely the truth is that no amount of training and development will turn some people into good leaders, whereas provided an individual has a minimum level of skill and knowledge, then his or her leadership skills can probably be enhanced. However, trait theories assume that if we cannot make good leaders we can at least select them. The kinds of traits identified as being essential for good leadership are:

- intelligence;
- courage;
- enthusiasm;
- perseverance;
- in some cases a 'helicopter quality', ie the ability to rise above a particular situation and view it in its entirety.

Theory X and theory Y

As we saw in Chapter 8, McGregor[2] stated that attitudes about the management role could be broadly divided into two categories, theory X and theory Y. Theory X is based on the following assumptions:

- the average human being has an inherent dislike of work and will avoid it if possible;
- because of this dislike of work most people have to be coerced and controlled to produce the effort required;
- the average human being prefers to be directed, wishes to avoid responsibility, has relatively little ambition and values security above all.

The assumptions of theory Y are that:

- effort put into work is as natural as rest or play;
- controls and punishments are not the only way of bringing about effort, and people will generally exercise self-control to achieve their objectives;
- how committed people are to objectives will depend on the reward associated with those objectives;
- the average human being will not only accept but also seek responsibility;
- the capacity for ingenuity and creativity in solving organisational problems is widespread;
- most people's potential is only being partly developed.

The implications of these assumptions for managers are clear. The theory X manager will believe in the 'carrot and stick' approach whereas the theory Y manager will seek to develop people and give them responsibilities.

Theory Z

To the above can be added what has been called 'Theory Z'. This is a

Japanese approach to management, proposed by Ouchi,[3] and it is characterised by:

- long-term and often lifetime employment;
- relatively slow appraisal and promotion;
- development of company-specific skills and specialisation;
- an emphasis on informal controls that are supported by a framework of more formal ones;
- decision making by consensus;
- collective decision making but with individual accountability;
- a general concern for employees and peers and for relationships within the organisation.

Perceived differences in Japanese and European culture and behaviour

A training programme at the Japan Travel Bureau identified the following differences between Japanese and European companies:

Japanese	European
Live to work	Work to live
Lifetime employment – commitment to one company	Lifetime employees but changing companies is acceptable
24-hour commitment	Life outside work
Seniority systems of advancement	Tendency to meritocracy
Reluctant to impose views – tendency to seek unity	Likely to impose personal opinions
Strong group orientation	Work in groups but have individual needs
Expect to give and receive quality of service	Difficulty in appreciating concepts of quality
Influenced by position and age	Influenced by personality and qualifications
Employees developed as company specialists	Functional specialism
Indirect in speech – can appear dishonest	Direct and can appear rude
Strong behavioural code covering etiquette	Less rigorous codes of behaviour
Slow decision-making, involving consultation	Fast decision-making
Swift implementation after decision is taken	Slow implementation

From Fitzgerald, J (1991) 'A Japanese lesson in European togetherness', *Personnel Management*, September.

A continuum of management styles

Management styles are often characterised as being at one end of an extreme, either autocratic, in which the manager tells his or her staff what to do and expects it to be done without argument, or democratic, in which there is full discussion before any decision is made. Tannenbaum and Schmidt[4] have described a continuum of management styles in which the area of freedom given to subordinates increases gradually from one end to the other. This ranges from a highly autocratic approach, in which the manager makes a decision and then tells people to implement it, through an approach in which the decision has to be sold to the individuals concerned using the manager's persuasive powers, to a situation in which subordinates are given substantial freedom to act within certain overall parameters. This process is illustrated in Figure 9.2.

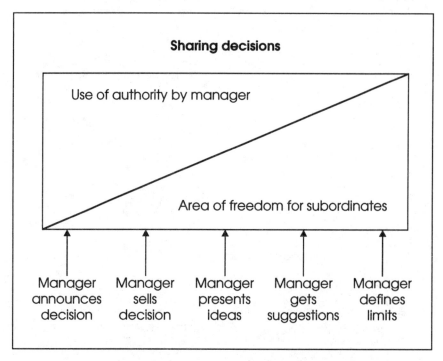

Figure 9.2 *A continuum of management styles*

The managerial grid

The managerial grid, devised by Blake and Mouton[5] and shown in Figure 9.3, depicts management style in terms of two dimensions:

- concern for production;
- concern for people.

Each axis goes from 1–9 and the position of a particular style of management can be plotted on the grid. In Figure 9.3 a 1.1 management style shows a low concern with both production and people. Managers at this level are likely to show little interest in either and to be unwilling to change.

1.9 managers are those who are very concerned about people but not so worried about results. Their attitude is that if people are happy they will produce the results anyway. Their main concern is for harmonious relationships and this can be an appropriate management style where objectives are social rather than based on output.

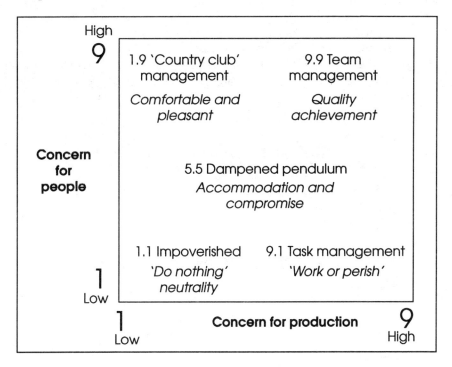

Figure 9.3   *The managerial grid*

The 9.1 managers, by contrast, have an almost total concern with tasks and are not too worried about how results are achieved. People come second and the 9.1 manager will adopt an autocratic approach and push hard to get results. There are situations in which such an approach might be appropriate, such as where it is essential to achieve results quickly and with minimum discussion.

The 5.5 management style is a middle-of-the-road approach in which the manager will try to compromise between the tasks that have to be done and issues of people.

The ideal on this grid is the 9.9 manager, who has a high concern for getting the task done but also for ensuring that people are committed to achieving results. This is the kind of approach which is considered to achieve high quality performance.

The Ohio State studies

The managerial grid described above has similarities to an approach developed by the Bureau of Business Research following studies undertaken at Ohio State University.[6] Here the focus was on two main aspects of management:

- *consideration* — meaning the extent to which the leader showed concern with the group and its members and worked towards gaining their trust and respect;
- *structure* — which reflected the extent to which the leader was concerned with goals and the way activities were organised to achieve those goals.

Management styles were described on the basis of the four different approaches described in Figure 9.4. In this approach the ideal management style, for most purposes, was one which demonstrated high consideration and high structure.

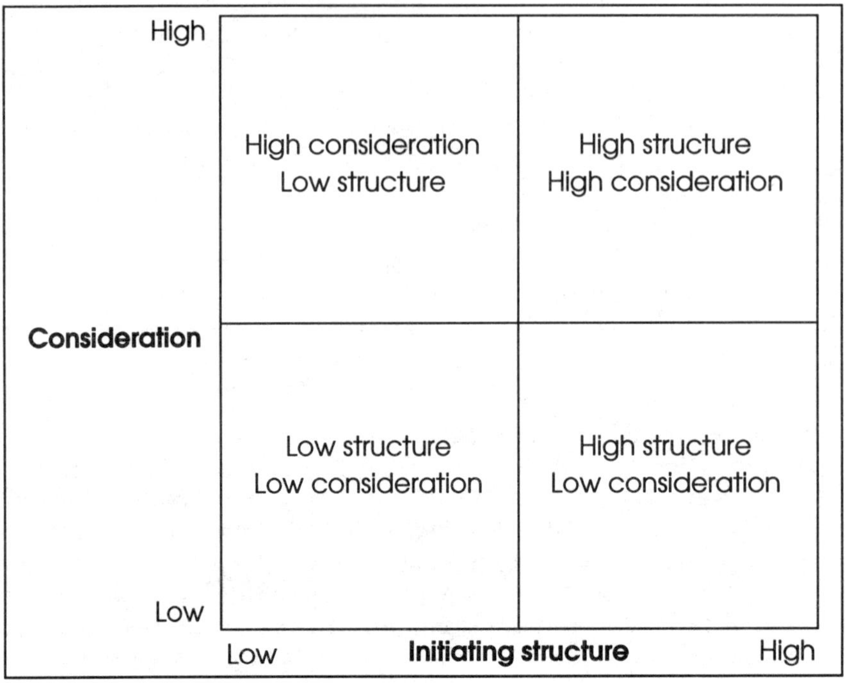

High consideration Low structure	High structure High consideration
Low structure Low consideration	High structure Low consideration

Consideration (vertical axis, High to Low)
Initiating structure (horizontal axis, Low to High)

Figure 9.4   *The Ohio State studies*

Reddin's 3D model

Reddin's model[7] takes the task and relationship orientations of the managerial grid and introduces a third element, effectiveness. From this he identified eight styles of management, four that were less effective and four that were more effective. Effectiveness means the appropriateness of a particular style to the circumstances in which it is applied. These styles are as follows:

Less effective styles	More effective styles
Deserter	Bureaucrat
Missionary	Developer
Autocrat	Benevolent autocrat
Compromiser	Executive

These styles are described in more detail below:

1. *Deserter* — a manager who shows a lack of interest in both tasks and relationships and is ineffective because of this and the resultant lowering of morale.
2. *Missionary* — this is someone who has a high concern for relationships but not for tasks. This person prefers failing to get things done rather than risking a disruption of harmony.
3. *Autocrat* — this person is primarily concerned about getting the work done and is unconcerned about the effect of his or her behaviour on relationships. Such a person may create fear in staff, who may therefore only work when they are bullied into it.
4. *Compromiser* — this is someone who is concerned about getting the job done and about relationships, but who is unwilling or unable to make strong decisions. He or she is therefore likely to equivocate and compromise, tending to take the line of least resistance, and will tend to focus on the pressures of the immediate situation at the expense of long-term objectives.
5. *Bureaucrat* — this describes the kind of person who is not really interested in the task or in relationships, but who by following the rules and applying procedures will be seen as conscientious.
6. *Developer* — this is someone who has a high concern for relationships and therefore places trust in people. His or her prime motivation is to develop the abilities of others and to achieve the maximum satisfaction and motivation. There is a

danger, however, in this approach that the high concern for relationships can mean that he or she might put individuals before the interests of the organisation.

7. *Benevolent autocrat* — this is someone who is more concerned about getting the job done than about relationships, but who has enough skill to get others to work effectively without causing resentment.

8. *Executive* — this is someone who has a high concern both for relationships and for getting the job done. This person sets high standards and treats people as individuals. This manager will be perceived as a good motivator and an effective team leader.

The path-goal theory

This is based on the theory that the performance of subordinates will depend on their perception of the rewards available, and is therefore related to the expectancy theory of motivation (see Chapter 8). The most effective managers will be those who are seen to be able to create the kinds of rewards that are of interest to subordinates.

Under this system the main factors affecting leadership behaviour will be the individual characteristics of subordinates and the nature of the work undertaken. The main practical problem is likely to be the extent to which the manager is able to provide the rewards desired. For example, promotion may well be a motivational factor for some subordinates but, particularly in a relatively flat organisation structure, there are unlikely to be enough promotion posts to satisfy everybody.

The Hersey and Blanchard situational leadership model

In this model Hersey and Blanchard[8] identified one of the main variables determining management style as the 'maturity' of the subordinates. Maturity in this context refers to the employees' degree of experience, ability and willingness to accept responsibility for a particular task. This is further divided into job maturity, referring to the individual's skills and experience, and psychological maturity, which refers to the individual's self-confidence and personal image. The implications of this are that a relatively inexperienced subordinate who lacks confidence may need a more directive style of management than one who has substantial experience and a high level of self-confidence.

This approach identifies four levels of subordinate readiness:

- R1 — low readiness, the followers are both unable and unwilling or insecure;
- R2 — low to moderate readiness, where the subordinates are unable but willing, or where they lack confidence;
- R3 — moderate to high readiness, where the subordinates are able but unwilling, or lack confidence in their ability to perform;
- R4 — high readiness, where the subordinates are both able and willing, or are confident of their ability.

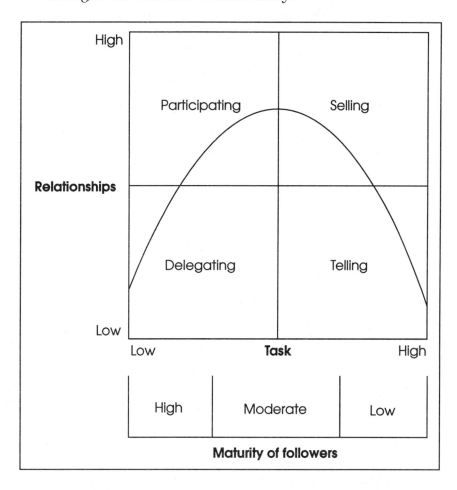

Figure 9.5 *The Hersey and Blanchard situational leadership model*

These stages of maturity are then plotted against an axis showing orientation towards one of the following:

- relationship behaviour in which the manager engages in two-way communication;
- task behaviour in which the manager focuses primarily on defining and setting goals.

This leads to four different leadership styles (see Figure 9.5):

- S1 — *telling*, in which there is a great deal of instruction given, which is a situation most appropriate to low subordinate readiness;
- S2 — *selling*, in which the manager explains the basis of decisions and gives clarification, which is suitable for subordinates at the R2 level;
- S3 — *participating*, in which the leader shares ideas and involves subordinates in the decision-making process, which is considered the most appropriate style for moderate to high readiness, ie R3;
- S4 — *delegating*, in which there is little direction given, with subordinates having the authority to take decisions and act on them, which is seen as appropriate only for mature subordinates with high readiness, ie R4.

Although this kind of approach does have the advantage of taking account of the different stages of development and abilities of subordinates, it does suffer from various disadvantages. There may be different interpretations of what constitutes maturity and it cannot cover all situations. In addition, insufficient weight is given to the nature of the task, and the organisation's structure, culture and climate are not really taken into account.

Likert's 4-fold model of management systems

Based on research, Likert[9] identified four different types of management. These he described as:

- System 1: Exploitative authoritative;
- System 2: Benevolent authoritative;
- System 3: Consultative;
- System 4: Participative group.

System 1 managers operate a style based on threats with little team work, and impose decisions on subordinates.

System 2 managers give subordinates some flexibility within certain limits, but other systems still remain fundamentally autocratic and based on rewards.

System 3 managers discuss decisions and goals with subordinates and encourage team work, although motivation is still primarily based on rewards.

System 4 managers show a high degree of trust and confidence in subordinates, with strong communication between both parties, a high degree of team work and rewards based on achievement of previously agreed goals.

Likert's general conclusion was that employees who adopted system 4 management styles were the most effective in terms of productivity, quality and overall efficiency.

The Hay McBer approach

The Hay McBer approach outlines six managerial styles that are likely to be more or less effective, depending on the circumstances. It is recognised that the effectiveness of any particular style will depend on a number of factors including the organisation's culture and climate, the nature and timing of the tasks to be achieved, and the social motives of the subordinates. These social motives relate to the individual's needs for achievement, affiliation and power.

The Hay McBer management styles are categorised as:

- *Coercive* — employees are told what to do and expected to get on with it.
- *Authoritative* — clear directions and explanations are given; a firm but fair approach.
- *Affiliative* — puts people first.
- *Democratic-participative* — seeks commitment through consensus.
- *Pace-setting* — shows how to do the job and sets high standards for others to follow.
- *Coaching* — seeks to develop others and views this as the manager's main role.

DETERMINING THE APPROPRIATE MANAGEMENT STYLE

All the above descriptions of management style are useful techniques for making individual managers think about how they should control and motivate their subordinates. The problem, however, is that all the theorists are trying to develop a model for what is a very complex situation. The reality is that no one style or mode of behaviour will suit all circumstances. The manager has to vary his or her style according to:

- the nature of the work to be carried out;
- the timescale for its completion;

- the number and types of subordinates managed;
- the knowledge, skills and experience of those subordinates;
- the nature of subordinates' attitudes and motivations;
- the type of organisation;
- the organisation structure and processes;
- the organisation climate and culture (although these will be influenced by management style);
- the environment, both internal and external;
- the manager's own perceptions and beliefs.

This list may not be exhaustive but it is intended to indicate just how complex the management role can be. Management style will have to be varied according to the individual and the situation. In any one group there may be people who like to be directed and told what to do, whereas there may be others who loathe it. Just to complicate matters further, the same person might want to be directed on one occasion but not on another. While a manager might usually adopt a highly participative management style, there may be occasions, for example when there is a rush job, when he or she may need to be directive just to complete the task on time.

In the UK armed forces, for example, there is a move towards a much more participative style of decision making. However, while this may work well in times of peace, there would not be time to seek consensus when troops are under fire. In such a situation commands would have to be issued and obeyed without question, instantly.

External factors can have an impact on management style, on individual motivation and on organisational climate. When business is good, it is easy to be optimistic and to put a great deal of emphasis on training and development. However, when times are hard and there is a threat of redundancy in the air, morale can plummet and at such times leadership may need to be much firmer to encourage a clear sense of direction and confidence.

MANAGEMENT SKILLS

Setting targets and getting results

The key role of the manager is to get results. This will only be achieved if subordinates are completely clear about what is expected of them. Part of the management role should be to respond to statements by subordinates such as:

- Tell me what you want me to do.

- Give me an opportunity to show how well I can perform.
- Tell me how I am doing.
- Give me guidance and support when I need it.
- Reward me according to my contribution.
- Give me equal treatment to the others in the group.

To satisfy the above requirements, the manager should adopt an approach which has the following elements:

1. The manager should be clear about the results he or she is expected to achieve. This should be agreed by discussion with the manager's boss.

2. The manager should then determine the individual results required from each member of the team and discuss with each person what is required in terms of outputs and standards of performance.

3. As part of the objective-setting process, the manager should help subordinates identify priorities or key result areas. There should be no more than 6–8 of these, as any more will be less likely to be priorities and will weaken the individual's focus on particular areas.

4. To ensure that the required level of performance is attained and to achieve improvement in key areas, the manager will need to help establish performance standards. Where possible these should be quantitative. Some examples are given below.

Key result area	Standards
1. Provide an acceptable level of customer service.	Respond to routine queries within 24 hours.
2. Maintain cash flow.	Despatch invoices within 1 week.
3. Reduce overhead costs.	Reduce overhead costs by 5% on the previous year's figure.

You will note that in the above example item 3 is an improvement target rather than just a performance standard.

5. Subordinates should be given regular feedback on performance, with coaching where required, and targets should be adjusted in the light of changed circumstances. Discussions with subordinates should form a regular part of the manager's

role, and will not only help to provide guidance, but will also be a means of gaining information and assessing progress.

6. Additional advice, training and development should be provided where required.
7. There should be a reward system that is fair and equitable and which, as far as possible, meets the needs of the people concerned. This certainly means having a pay structure which adequately rewards job size and individual performance.

All the above should be incorporated in a comprehensive performance management system which should include:

- planning the work and deciding on objectives;
- managing subordinates' performance on a continual basis;
- formal review of performance at regular intervals through two-way appraisal interviews;
- rewarding people according to their performance, provided this can be objectively assessed.

There are many techniques and approaches the manager will need to apply. For example, there will need to be job descriptions outlining the key accountabilities of each job (not just a list of tasks to be carried out), the key performance indicators, performance standards, performance statistics and so on (see Chapter 6).

DELEGATION

We have already said that the management role involves getting work done through others. This means trying to ensure that work is done at the lowest level which is competent to do it. Not only does this make sound economic sense, since there is no point in employing highly paid professionals to undertake straightforward routine work, but it is also likely to give people a greater sense of job satisfaction. Most people like to feel that they are in control of their work and have some decision-making authority. Delegation is therefore fundamental for effective management and is central to the concept of empowerment considered in Chapter 7.

Delegation also has other advantages:

1. It gives a manager time to think and plan ahead.
2. It helps to develop skills in others, which is essential to achieve flexibility and for management succession.
3. It enables greater use to be made of the specialist skills within the team.
4. As indicated above, individuals are more likely to feel committed to tasks for which they are accountable.

Problems with delegation

The problems with delegation are the following:

1. There is a degree of risk as individuals may have to learn through mistakes. However, this risk can be minimised by careful planning and clear instructions.
2. Many managers often feel that by delegating they are somehow losing control and will not really know what is happening.
3. Some managers feel that they could delegate themselves out of a job, and will be more likely to retain work that could be passed down in order to justify their existence.
4. A degree of comfort can often be derived from work which is familiar, and there may genuinely be technical parts of the job that the manager likes to do.
5. Delegation can be time consuming in the initial stages because there will need to be a great deal of explanation, coaching and progress reviews.
6. Most managers probably feel that they can do the job better than anyone else.
7. As knowledge is one source of power, some managers feel that by allowing their subordinates more freedom they themselves might be undermined, or be overtaken by those subordinates.

Other factors affecting delegation

The ability of the manager to delegate will be affected by many factors, including:

*   the type of organisation and the work carried out;
*   the timescales in which results have to be achieved — there may just not be time to explain what needs to be done;
*   the abilities and experience of subordinates;
*   the span of control of the manager;
*   the existing workload of the team might be such that delegation is not practical.

How to delegate

Delegation is not easy. To carry it out effectively you need to go through the following stages:

1. Examine your own workload and behaviour to see if there is anything you could pass down. Consider in particular whether you are becoming involved in too much detail, spending too

much time checking people's work, or working longer hours than you should.

2. Plan what you can delegate. This will involve looking at your own job, breaking it down into its component parts and selecting the key areas that you must concentrate on.
3. Write down the time spent on each activity.
4. Identify the components of the job which you have to do yourself.
5. Focus particularly on routine and time-consuming tasks.
6. Review the experience and capabilities of your staff to determine which areas could be effectively handed over.
7. Hand over those areas that you feel can be delegated, giving clear instructions and any necessary training to the people concerned.

Conclusion

The management role is a vital but complex one. It is probably the factor above all others that makes the real difference between business success and failure. There have been many attempts to try to explain and categorise different management styles, but in many respects it is tempting to think that it really all comes back to the quality of the individual, which sounds very much like the trait approach mentioned earlier in this chapter. Indeed, there has been a return, of late, to this kind of approach.

In practical terms, anyone occupying a management role, whether or not he or she possesses the desired or essential traits, can only try to perform effectively as a manager. This includes monitoring and assessing his or her own performance on a regular basis. Reproduced in the box opposite are at least some of the questions the manager should ask himself/herself for this purpose.

The manager as leader

The leadership role involves being:

- the top co-ordinator for the team or group;
- the planner of the group's activities;
- the developer of the group's policies;
- the person who gives rewards and imposes sanctions;
- the group's representative to others;
- the group's chief conciliator and negotiator;
- the provider of advice and support;
- a source of expert information and ideas;
- the main communicator of the organisation's policies;
- the group's main trainer/developer;
- a unifying force;
- an example of the kinds of behaviour expected.

A manager's checklist

1. Are you clear about your objectives?
2. Are you clear about what tasks need to be carried out to achieve these objectives?
3. Are the members of your team clear about what is required of them?
4. Are all the tasks undertaken essential?
5. Is there any way in which processes could be improved?
6. Do you give all members of your team clear and honest feedback about their performance?
7. Do you know the strengths and weaknesses of your team members?
8. Is all the work you carry out essential or could some of it be delegated?
9. Do you have the right numbers and types of people in your team to achieve the required results?
10. Do you know what the training requirements of individual team members are?

References

[1] Adair, J (1979) *Action Centred Leadership*, Gower, London.
[2] McGregor, D M (1960) *The Human Side of Enterprise*, McGraw-Hill, New York.
[3] Ouchi, W G (1981) *Theory Z: How American business can meet the Japanese challenge*, Addison-Wesley, Reading, MA.
[4] Tannenbaum, R and Schmidt, W H (1973) 'How to choose a leadership pattern', *Harvard Business Review*, May–June.
[5] Blake, R B and Mouton, J S (1964) *The Management Grid*, Gulf Publishing Co, Houston.
[6] Fleishman, E A (1974) 'Leadership climate, human relations training and supervisory behaviour' in Fleishman, E A and Bass, A T *Studies in Personnel and Industrial Psychology*, 3rd edn, Dorsey, Homewood, Illinois.
[7] Reddin, W J (1970) *Managerial Effectiveness*, McGraw-Hill, New York.
[8] Hersey, P and Blanchard, K (1988) *Management of Organizational Behaviour*, 5th edn, Prentice-Hall, New Jersey.
[9] Likert, R (1971) *New Patterns of Management*, McGraw-Hill, New York.

Communication

T his chapter considers the issue of communication in organisations and attempts to:

- define what is meant by communication;
- describe barriers to effective communication;
- consider specific types of communication;
- suggest ways in which communication can be made more effective.

DEFINITION

Communication may be regarded as effective when the ideas and intentions of one person are successfully conveyed to another. The problem is that, as we do not usually have the advantage of telepathy, our thoughts and ideas have to be expressed in some form of code, that is the language we use or our physical movements and gestures, or 'body language' as it is commonly known.

The communication process is sometimes described in terms of transmitters and receivers, with a certain amount of interference between the two. This 'interference' represents the barriers to effective communication described below (see Figure 10.1).

Communication has a number of purposes, which include:

- sharing information;
- considering ideas;
- transmitting and exchanging opinions;
- transmitting feelings.

The need to communicate arises from our need for social interaction to achieve certain results. Effective communication is essential at all levels in any organisation to ensure that it functions effectively and meets its goals.

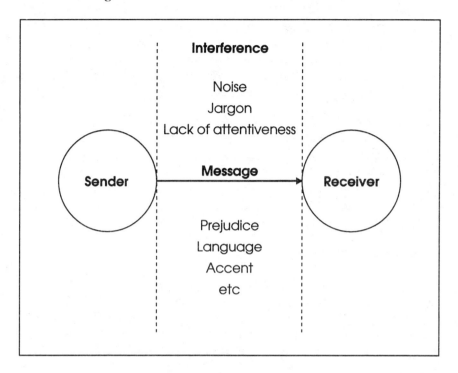

Figure 10.1 *Some barriers to communication*

BARRIERS TO COMMUNICATION

Barriers to communication can come from a number of sources. The problem may be with the sender of the message, who may be unable, or indeed unwilling, to communicate the necessary message very clearly; or with the receiver, who for various reasons may be unable or unwilling to understand the message being sent; or there may be environmental factors affecting the conditions under which the message is conveyed, such as noise.

There is also a tendency on the part of many people to assume that once the message has been sent it has automatically been received. Most people have experienced the kind of situation in which a memorandum may be sent out to employees, but for various reasons it is not acted on. All too often managers assume that the act of sending the communication is sufficient to guarantee action. They should, however, check to ensure that the message has

Some of the major barriers to communication are considered in more detail below.

Poor communication skills

The sender of any particular message may not be particularly articulate either verbally or in writing, and will therefore fail to convey the information accurately.

Emotional state

The current emotional state of the sender or the receiver of any message will affect the way that message is perceived. Someone who has particularly strong emotions on a particular topic may not listen very clearly and certainly not very objectively to what is said on that topic.

Language and words used

The kind of language and words used will have a major effect on the success of any communication. A person's accent may be less clear to some people than others. The words and expressions used are also likely to have different meanings for different people. The expression 'trade union', for example, will produce different reactions in different people. The point is that the meaning of words is inside us, not in the words themselves. Similarly, the use of jargon or slang might have meaning for some people but not for others.

Message distortion

Most people are familiar with the effects of chain messages. As a verbal message is passed from one person to another, it becomes more and more distorted. In organisations this means that long lines of command will mean a message is more likely to be distorted in transit. Senior managers can quickly become out of touch with those at the 'sharp end' in large organisations and may not only lose credibility with staff, but also lose touch with the requirements of their customers. For this reason, relatively flat structures with fewer organisational levels are generally regarded as better environments for communication and decision making.

Preoccupation

When the receiver of a particular message is preoccupied with other matters, the content of the message being sent may not be fully appreciated. This is likely to be particularly the case when the message is uninteresting or unwelcome. No doubt everyone has experienced a situation in which they have switched off mentally, but continued to make the expected noises of encouragement or assent to the sender of the message. It may be difficult to concentrate in a lecture when your third cup of coffee is beginning to make its presence felt!

Information overload

Many messages get lost because of the sheer volume of information being passed to the receiver. When someone receives too many internal memoranda on relatively trivial issues, the important messages may get lost unless special attention is drawn to them in some way. One of the symptoms of an organisation under stress is an increase in paperwork as it strives to reinforce important messages about such things as cash flow and profitability, and also as people try to demonstrate that they are pulling their weight. However, there is the danger that the sheer volume of paper will mean that important messages might be lost in a flow of trivia.

Hostility

Where there is hostility between the sender and the receiver of a message, or hostility about the subject matter itself, the message is likely to be distorted to provide ammunition which reinforces existing attitudes.

Past experience

Where an individual feels that the sender of a particular message has nothing worthwhile to say, based perhaps on previous experience, or for example when past meetings have proved to be a waste of time, expectations are likely to be low and little attention will be paid to what is said.

Status of message sender

Where the sender of the message is a person of high status or standing or has a charismatic personality, the message is more likely to be listened to. On the other hand, people holding senior positions in an organisation may sometimes find it difficult to communicate with those lower down the structure, as such people may be unwilling to discuss the true position or their particular feelings. Some may feel threatened and act defensively, while others may be hostile to senior managers.

Defensiveness

People may often feel threatened by particular questions, especially at meetings. This can mean that they are more interested in camouflage and avoiding giving direct answers to questions than in communicating the truth.

Stereotyping

Stereotyping involves the adoption of a fixed idea about how members of any specific group will be expected to behave. This is particularly true of racial stereotypes, for example, when any person may be assumed to have all the characteristics associated with his or her particular race. This can affect the perception of that person's statements or behaviour.

The halo effect

The halo effect occurs when, because of certain characteristics shown by a person, we assume that he or she possesses a whole range of other characteristics which seem appropriate. For example, it may well be assumed that someone who speaks particularly well is also intelligent, hardworking, tenacious and so on. This may well all be true but it is, nevertheless, making assumptions based on the limited evidence of one particular characteristic. Unfortunately, this is all too often what can happen in selection interviews if they are unsupported by other approaches.

Hidden agenda

At virtually any meeting, those attending will have aims other than those for which the meeting has been convened. For example, people who are at a meeting attended by their boss are likely to want to give a favourable impression and may therefore make statements calculated to do just that. Certainly, the most successful people in many organisations are those who are adept at impression management, that is conveying just the kind of image that they know to be favoured by the organisation's managers.

Attentiveness and listening skills

The effectiveness of any communication will be greatly affected by a person's listening skills, ie the ability to concentrate on what is being said and to understand the meaning of the words, and the extent to which he or she feels inclined to listen carefully to what is being said. Unfortunately, all too many people will hear only what they want to hear and read only what they want to read.

Group attitudes

The membership of a particular reference group, that is a group to which a person closely relates, will influence his or her attitude to any communication received. Such a group may, for example, be a political party, a particular religion, or a certain profession. This is vividly demonstrated by the 'group think' attitudes discussed in Chapter 7.

Physical environment

The physical environment can affect the quality of communication. If there is, for example, a great deal of noise, then it will be hard to hear what people are saying. Lecture rooms that are overcrowded, warm and stuffy make it difficult to concentrate on what is being said. Not for nothing is the dreaded after lunch slot on any course or seminar known as the 'graveyard session'.

METHODS OF COMMUNICATION

There are a number of ways of communicating in an organisation, the most important of which are:

- meetings and face-to-face discussions;
- internal circulars and memoranda;
- telephone conversations;
- electronic mail;
- the notice-board.

These are considered in turn below.

Meetings and discussions

The word 'meeting' can cover a whole range of different types of event, from an informal chat between two people to a highly structured conference of several hundred. Some meetings may have few rules and no formal agenda, whereas others, such as formally constituted committees, will have a written agenda, formal rules of procedure and agreed minutes.

Meetings may be held for a number of purposes, such as:

- *Giving information* — for example, where a manager may need to explain targets or changes in procedure.
- *Collecting information* — for example, where a manager requires information from subordinates and colleagues before a decision can be made.
- *Explaining decisions* — where a manager might go beyond merely informing people about decisions but will discuss them in more depth, seek feedback and give further detailed explanations.
- *Problem solving* — where all those gathered at the meeting are there to try to resolve an issue or a problem and every member will be expected to contribute to the discussion. Such meetings need to be organised in a way that encourages people to express views and ideas without censure.
- *Joint consultation and negotiation* — where the object of the exercise is to arrive at an agreement about an issue that is acceptable to both sides. Such meetings are typical in unionised organisations and are characterised by having two sides representing the main differences of opinion, but with a certain amount of give and take.

Meetings are often criticised for being a poor way of reaching decisions ('a camel is a horse designed by a committee'). Usually decisions are taken either by majority vote, if the meeting is a formal one, or by consensus, if the meeting is more informal. The problem with consensus decision making is that very often there is assumed to be a general agreement which may not, in reality, exist.

Meetings are subject to a number of influences which can adversely affect the quality of decisions made, including, for example:

- all the barriers to communication mentioned above;
- domination by one or two powerful people;
- a tendency to take more risky decisions;
- in close-knit, highly cohesive groups, a tendency to take decisions that are very introspective and ignore external influences;
- less assertive members of the meeting may not have their views adequately considered.

There is often a suspicion that meetings are convened and committees established to avoid taking decisions on difficult issues. Certainly this does happen. In one particular company a committee was set up to develop a career progression scheme for the organisation. This committee included representatives of all the main professions in the organisation, of which there were several, as well as trade union representatives. No one group of professionals wanted to see any of the others gaining an advantage in pay terms, and the consequence was that this group kept meeting for more than five years without reaching a consensus decision. Job evaluation panels can often fall into the same trap. Many schemes have a 'sore-thumbing' stage, at which managers from the organisation consider whether the job evaluation results are a fair reflection of their perception of job sizes in the organisation. If these meetings are not carefully constituted and controlled, they can soon degenerate into battles for supremacy between departments and professions.

Despite the above problems, meetings are essential and indispensable. The important thing is to ensure that they are convened for a purpose and that they are effectively managed. This is discussed further below.

Circulars and memoranda

One of the most common ways of communicating information in an organisation is by sending out a circular or an internal memorandum. The advantages of conveying information this way are that:

- by putting the message in writing, provided it is clearly written, there should be no misunderstanding about the content of the message;
- by putting it in writing the sender of the message is leaving nothing to chance;
- sending out a circular enables a lot of people to be contacted in a short space of time;
- there is less chance of the message becoming distorted than if the communication were undertaken verbally.

There are, however, also a number of disadvantages:

- internal circulars and memoranda often get ignored, especially if the organisation is in the habit of sending out a large number;
- communication in this way does not give the receiver of the message the opportunity to note the subtleties of tones of voice or body language and therefore, particularly where there is a need to read between the lines, the message may not be fully comprehended;
- there can often be a tendency on the part of the sender of such messages to feel that sending the message is the same as taking action;

- the effectiveness of the message depends very much on the writing skill of the sender.

Telephone conversations

The telephone is obviously one of the most useful and quickest ways of communicating with other people, particularly at remote locations. Telephone conversations have the advantages of:

- speed;
- the ability to convey meaning by tone of voice;
- the ability to get immediate feedback on any message and discuss its implications;
- adaptability, as topics other than the immediate reason for the call can also be discussed.

The disadvantages are:

- telephone conversations are not really suitable for conveying more complex messages and might, in any case, have to be confirmed in writing;
- there is usually no evidence that the conversation has actually taken place, so this is open to manipulation;
- because there is no face-to-face meeting the recipient of the call cannot take account of the caller's body language;
- such conversations are usually hedged with certain social conventions, such as asking if the caller enjoyed a recent holiday, and might include discussions not relevant to the subject in question, thereby wasting time;
- many people are nervous about or not very good at using the telephone and may therefore not convey the right message.

The grapevine

The difference between the grapevine and the other forms of communication mentioned is that it is an unofficial and informal method of communication. However, we all know how quickly information can be passed in this way. The main drawback is that information obtained on the grapevine is more likely to be rumour than fact, and it can therefore have a potentially harmful effect on the organisation. There are also occasions when managers might use the grapevine for their own ends, to convey information that they cannot pass through the usual official channels.

To counteract any potentially harmful effects of the grapevine, managers need to ensure that the organisation's messages are passed on very clearly and promptly. If employees feel that managers are concealing information likely to affect them, the grapevine will flourish.

Fax machines

The use of fax machines is becoming more common and they are a speedy way of conveying important information. While a fax has most of the same advantages and disadvantages of a circular, the main difference is that this kind of communication is usually used relatively infrequently and only for urgent messages. It is, therefore, a powerful means of ensuring that a message is given instant attention.

Notice-board

The notice-board is useful for general, low-key communication, such as informing staff about sports and social activities, but should not be relied on to communicate important information as it is likely to be ignored by most people. Notice-boards will be read only if the information is up to date and of some interest to the employees concerned. Provided these conditions are met, notice-boards can be used to support other communications.

Electronic mail

The use of electronic mail is becoming more common but is still not used as widely as it could be. Even where the facility exists it sometimes remains unused. While, therefore, it provides a possibly effective way of communicating important messages quickly, the organisation needs to ensure that everyone is trained and encouraged in its use.

HOW TO COMMUNICATE EFFECTIVELY

This section focuses on some ways in which communication may be made more effective. We consider, firstly, the general principles and then describe three particular areas: speaking, listening and conducting effective meetings.

Some general principles for effective communication

1. Be clear about the message you want to convey and the reason

for the message, for example to inform, to amuse, to seek information and so on.

2. Select the appropriate method of communication, having regard to content, timescale and target audience.
3. Prepare the message in the appropriate format and language, having particular regard to the nature and background of the people to be communicated with.
4. Where possible use more than one means of communication to reinforce the message and be prepared to repeat it if necessary.
5. Try to ensure that the sender of the message is someone with credibility in the organisation — a message from someone in the chief executive's office is unlikely to carry the same weight as a personal message from the chief executive.
6. Consider what is in it for those the message is for and highlight the benefits of any particular suggestion.
7. Give examples, where appropriate, to support the message.
8. Try to give factual information and careful explanations where required.
9. Structure any argument logically, working up to the conclusion.
10. Use any points you know people will agree with to reinforce your statements.
11. Try to ensure that you make the message as interesting as possible.
12. Test out your proposed message and take account of any constructive feedback.

Speaking effectively

Similar considerations to those set out above apply, although there are also some specific recommendations when speaking in public. These are:

1. As above, be clear about your message and what you want to achieve.
2. Get to know your audience and tailor your presentation to their needs.
3. Try to anticipate likely questions and objections.
4. Learn your material thoroughly and have all the relevant information available for reference.
5. Consider the alternative arguments and be prepared to discuss them.
6. Prepare any necessary notes — it is better to speak from notes than to read a prepared script.

7. Test how much time you require and stick to the timetable.
8. Check all facilities and any equipment you may be likely to use.
9. Ensure that visual aids are readable, clear and support the points you are making.
10. Prepare handouts for distribution.
11. Ensure that any presentation is logically structured with a beginning, a middle and an end. A sound format would be:
    - introduction of all concerned with the presentation;
    - aims of the presentation;
    - a statement of what you are going to talk about and how questions will be dealt with;
    - delivery of the presentation;
    - summary and conclusions;
    - questions.

    In addition, your delivery should have impact and gain people's attention. The conclusion should in some way link back to the opening.
12. Develop presentation skills. This area requires practice and training.

Effective listening

There are a number of habits that can be developed to improve listening skills. The main rules are:

1. Keep an open mind and do not decide beforehand that the person speaking has nothing worthwhile to say. Instead, try to evaluate the quality of the arguments advanced objectively.
2. Think ahead, but without interrupting, to evaluate whether the words actually used by the speaker say what you were expecting them to say.
3. Summarise what has been said whenever possible, to ensure that you have really understood the point being made.
4. Look at the speaker, to pick up any non-verbal communication.
5. Look beyond the words actually used to try to gauge the thoughts of the speaker. Words can sometimes get in the way of the meaning.

MEETINGS

Meetings are an inevitable consequence of running any organisation. They can range from the informal two person face-to-face chat, to the formal committee or board meeting with an agenda, minutes and rules of procedure. They remain one of the most commonly used ways of communicating and receiving information, discussing ideas and views, resolving problems and making decisions. At their best they can be highly productive and very effective mechanisms for assisting in the running of the organisation. At their worst, they can be divisive, point-scoring slanging matches with no real purpose. The one certainty is that meetings are here to stay. They give their members the opportunity to explore views and issues with colleagues in a situation where there is both verbal and non-verbal communication.

They provide an opportunity to let off steam up to a point. They usually provide their members with some degree of psychological satisfaction. However, they must not be allowed to degenerate into a pointless routine ('we always meet on Monday morning, whether or not there is anything to discuss'). Some rules for more effective meetings are suggested below.

Rules for effective meetings

1. Only hold the meeting if there is a reason for it.
2. Ensure that everyone knows the time, date and venue, and that any key people are able to attend.
3. Ensure that the venue and accommodation chosen are suitable in terms of size, availability, accessibility, comfort and facilities.
4. Consider how the furniture in the meeting room should be laid out, as this can have an effect on how the meeting will be conducted. In Figure 10.2 two very common types of seating arrangement are shown. Layout A is probably the most common, but it does suffer from a number of disadvantages:

    —   if the table is a particularly long one, those at the end may have difficulty in catching the Chairman's eye or in hearing what he or she says;
    —   those nearest the Chairman can sometimes be in a blind spot as there is a tendency to look more towards the middle;
    —   where the meeting is one of two sides, such as in a joint management/trade union meeting, there is a tendency for each to sit on a different side of the table. This can encourage eyeball-to-eyeball confrontation, with the table acting as a real barrier to communication. It is better to seat opponents next to each other as it is more difficult to argue with someone sitting next to you.

— the arrangement has a hierarchical feel to it, with the Chairman clearly being in control. While this can reinforce the authority of the Chairman, it might intimidate others.

Layout B avoids many of the problems outlined above. There are no sides and everyone has an equal position and opportunity for interaction. It generally encourages a more informal exchange of views.

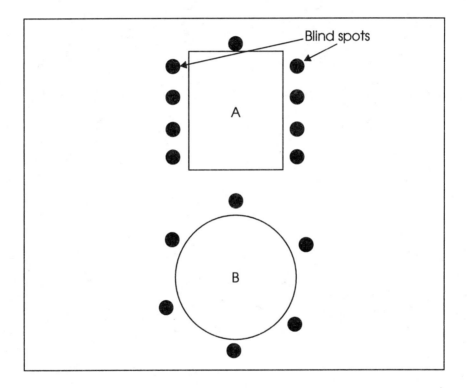

Figure 10.2 *Common seating arrangements*

5. Prepare an agenda, or at least have a specific objective for the meeting. If necessary put a time limit against each item. Distinguish between matters that are urgent and those that are important.
6. Give careful consideration to the numbers and types of people attending and the implications; for example if you invite a boss and his or her subordinate, will the latter talk freely?

7. If you are chairing the meeting, consider the best way of doing so and ensure that the meeting is properly structured and everyone contributes, that weaker members are protected, impetus is maintained and decisions are reached.

8. Summarise when any important decision is reached and at the end of the meeting.

9. Produce minutes or notes of the meeting with names against agreed actions.

10. Act on the decisions reached.

Glossary

Activity profiling Also known as activity analysis, this is a technique for measuring the relative benefits of activities undertaken by an organisation against their relative costs.

Alienative commitment This is one of the types of behaviour described by Etzioni, that is shown by people in certain organisations when they are unsympathetic to the aims of that organisation.

Assessment centres Assessment centres comprise a range of varied tests and exercises, perhaps including interviews, group discussions, in-tray exercises, psychometric and other written tests, sometimes conducted over a number of days, usually to assess suitability for appointment or promotion. When used for management development they are usually called development centres.

Brainstorming This is a group technique designed to elicit the highest number of ideas in the shortest possible time.

Bureaucratic organisation Bureaucracy was a term first coined by Weber to describe a certain type of organisation that was based on clearly defined roles and procedures. However, over the years it has developed a more negative connotation and now usually refers to an organisation that has unnecessarily cumbersome decision-making procedures.

Business process re-engineering Also known as value chain analysis, this describes an approach that fundamentally re-examines the organisation's processes to ensure that they are appropriate to the needs of the organisation's customers, and if necessary changes the existing strategy and structure to support key processes. The aim is to identify those that are strategically important.

Calculative commitment This is a type of behaviour described by Etzioni in which an individual is involved with an organisation because of the extrinsic (see below) rewards available. Commitment is likely to be low or negative.

Charismatic organisation   An organisation in which authority is derived from the outstanding personal qualities of the leader.

Coercive power   Organisational power that is exercised through the use of threats or sanctions.

Democratic organisation   This type of organisation is one in which there is substantial discussion on any decision before it is taken and where decision taking is widely spread throughout the organisation.

Differentation   A term used by Lawrence and Lorsch to describe the different behaviours of managers in terms of goal-setting, planning horizons, management style and inter-personal relations, and the degree of formality in the organisation structure.

Empowerment   A currently popular term which usually refers to the increased involvement of individuals throughout the structure in the decision-making process to increase their commitment and encourage the use of initiative. The leading exponent is Rosabeth Moss Kanter who has also highlighted the importance of empowerment for releasing the potential of women in particular.

Extrinsic rewards   Rewards derived from doing work that are not inherent in the work itself, eg pay.

Forming   A recognised first stage of group development when the members first begin to find out about each other. At this stage members are likely to be hesitant and nervous.

Group norms   Patterns of behaviour and rules established by a particular group to which all members are expected to conform. These can be stated or implied.

Group think   A situation in which all members of a particular group share common views, attitudes and beliefs, which are reinforced by the group members, leading to the danger of bad decisions being made because all outside ideas are rejected or ignored.

Inputs   Inputs in this context refers to the resources that come into an organisation before being converted into outputs.

Integration   This is a term used by Lawrence and Lorsch to describe the degree of co-operation and co-ordination between different parts of an organisation.

Intrinsic rewards These are the rewards that are inherent in a particular job, such as interesting work.

Inter-accountability matrix A means, devised by Hay, of comparing different jobs to identify any duplication or omissions in accountabilities.

Maintenance organisation A term used by Katz and Khan to describe organisations the principal aim of which is the socialisation of their members, such as schools.

Management style The usual pattern of behaviour demonstrated by a manager in the management of staff. It describes the techniques and relationship approaches used by the manager in getting results.

Mechanistic structure This is a term coined by Burns and Stalker to describe an organisation structured on the basis of clear and distinct tasks and a strong hierarchy, not unlike Weber's bureaucracy model. This structure was described as being more appropriate to stable, unchanging conditions, being characterised by slow decision-making processes. They contrasted this with organismic structures (see below).

Mission statement A statement of the organisation's fundamental purpose or philosophy.

Moral commitment This refers to one of the basic types of commitment identified by Etzioni in which members of the organisation support it because they believe in its aims. Morale and motivation is consequently likely to be high.

Motivation Motivation refers to the drives that make people behave in a particular way and strive to attain certain goals.

Normative power Power that derives from the general acceptance of the beliefs of the organisation, as in a political party.

Norming The stage of group formation during which group co-operation builds up and roles are taken by the various group members. Initial conflicts have been resolved by this stage.

Organigram (or organigramme) Another term for the organisation chart or family tree that shows the formal reporting lines in an organisation.

Organisation structure The reporting lines or chain of command in an organisation. The official or formal structure is that normally described on an organisation chart, whereas the informal structure is who reports to whom unofficially.

Organisation culture   The values and beliefs that are central to the organisation.

Organisation climate   This describes what it feels like to work for the organisation. It is the sum total of the feelings and attitudes of people who work there.

Organisational behaviour   The way individuals and groups behave in the organisation and the effect of this on the way the organisation is structured and managed.

Organisational design   This describes how the different elements of the organisation fit together and how they can be changed.

Organismic structure   This is a term coined by Burns and Stalker to describe a relatively loose, flexible and non-hierarchical type of organisation structure. The emphasis is more on the organisation's objectives, with strong lateral communications and a network structure. This kind of structure, in contrast to the mechanistic structure, was more appropriate to changing conditions and encouraged swift decision-making.

Outputs   What the organisation produces from its inputs.

Overlayering   Having more layers of management in the organisation's structure than are strictly necessary for operational efficiency and effectiveness.

Performing   The fourth and final stage of group development when initial conflicts have been resolved and the group is able to focus on solving problems and is able to reach decisions acceptable to the group.

Psychometric tests   Structured tests designed to measure abilities or capacities of individuals.

Remunerative power   Power exercised through the use of rewards or by control of resources.

Right-sizing   A technique developed by Hay to determine the appropriate manning levels for particular levels of service.

Role overload and role underload   Role overload means having too many roles to carry out or trying to meet conflicting expectations. Role underload generally arises when someone does not have a role that is sufficiently demanding in terms of his or her ability and experience.

Role-set   The combination of other roles with which one particular role interacts, eg colleagues.

Scalar chain A term coined by Fayol to describe the organisation's chain of command or reporting line.

Sociogram A means, devised by Moreno, of recording the frequency of interactions within a group.

Span of control The number of subordinates directly supervised.

Storming The second stage of group development during which arguments and conflicts arise as people seek to establish themselves within the group. Likely to be a noisy and emotional phase.

SWOT analysis An analysis of the strengths, weaknesses, opportunities and threats of an organisation, based on approaches devised by Ansoff.

T-groups Unstructured training groups involving leaderless discussions designed to improve individuals' understanding of their own motivations and behaviour.

Task specialisation The division of work operations into small components so that individual workers can achieve high levels of speed, skill and productivity.

Traditional organisation This is an organisation in which authority is established by custom and long-standing belief.

Unity of command One of the principles of organisation proposed by Fayol meaning a situation in which each post reports only to one other post.

Value for money (VFM) Value for money refers to an approach principally used by accountancy firms to review the efficiency, effectiveness and economy of organisations. This is an approach promoted by the Audit Commission for use in the public sector although the principles apply to any environment.

Zero-based budgeting A management tool in which budgets are annually justified from a zero base rather than by taking the previous year's figure and just updating it to allow for inflation. ZBB forces managers to question their assumptions and to identify and justify priorities.

Further Reading

Chapter 1   An Introduction to Organisational Behaviour and Design

Good introductory texts to the general area of organisational behaviour and design are:

Handy, CB (1976) *Understanding Organizations*, Penguin, Harmondsworth.

Mullins, LJ (1989) *Management and Organisational Behaviour*, 2nd edition, Pitman, London.

Pugh, DS and DJ Hickson (1989) *Writers on Organizations*, 4th edition, Penguin, Harmondsworth.

Pugh, DS (ed) (1990) *Organization Theory*, Penguin, Harmondsworth.

One of the leading founders of systems theory was Ludwig von Bertalanffy. See:

Bertalanffy, L (1972) 'The History and Status of General Systems Theory', *Academy of Management Journal*, vol 15, No 4.

Chapter 2   Classification of Organisations

In addition to the methods of analysis described in this chapter it is also worth reading publications by what is described as the Aston Group, based at the University of Aston in Birmingham. The Aston Programme studied 46 diverse organisations in the Birmingham area and analysed their organisation structures in terms of:

- specialization of roles and functions;
- standardization of procedures;
- formalization of documentation;
- centralization of authority;
- configuration of role structure.

See:

Pugh, DS, Hickson, DJ, Hinings, CR and Turner, C (1968) 'Dimensions of Organization Structure', *Administrative Science Quarterly*, vol 13, June.

Chapter 3   *Organisational Analysis*

SWOT analysis is generally regarded as having been developed from Ansoff. See:

Ansoff, HI (1987) *Corporate Strategy*, revised edition, Penguin, Harmondsworth.

On organisation culture read:

Hofstede, G 'Motivation, Leadership and Organization: Do American Theories Apply Abroad?', reprinted in Pugh, DS (ed) (1990) *Organization Theory*, Penguin, Harmondsworth.
Schein, E (1980) *Organizational Psychology*, Prentice-Hall, New Jersey.
Schein, E (1985) *Organizational Culture and Leadership*, Jossey-Bass, San Francisco, Ca.

For general information on financial analysis see:

Bowlin, OD, Martin JD, Scott, DF (1980) *Guide to Financial Analysis*, McGraw-Hill, New York.
Reid, W and Myddelton, DR (1985), *The Meaning of Company Accounts*, 3rd edition, Gower, Aldershot.
Warren, R (1983) *How to Understand and Use Company Accounts*, Business Books, London.

For information on statistical analysis read:

Daniel, WW and Terrell, JC (1975) *Business Statistics — Basic Concepts and Methodology*, Houghton Mifflin, Boston.
Emory, CW (1976) *Business Research Methods*, Irwin, Homewood, Illinois.
Harnett, DL (1982) *Statistical Methods*, Addison-Wesley, Reading, Mass.

Regarded by many as the leading authority on strategies for securing competitive advantage in organisations, and a major proponent of value chain analysis, or business process re-engineering, is Michael Porter. His major books are:

Porter, ME (1980) *Competitive Strategy: Techniques for Analysing Industries and Competitors*, Free Press, New York.
Porter, ME (1985) *Competitive Advantage*, Free Press, New York.
Porter, ME (1990) *The Competitive Advantage of Nations*, Macmillan, London.

For information on systems analysis read:

Ein-Dor, P and Jones, CR (1985) *Information Systems Management: Analytical Tools and Techniques*, North-Holland, Amsterdam.
Gane, T and Sarson, T (1985) *Structured Systems Analysis: Tools and Techniques*, McDonnell Douglas, St Louis, Mo.

Chapter 4   Mission and Strategy

Most of the authors mentioned under the other chapter headings refer to mission and strategy. However, particularly relevant are most books by Ansoff, Handy, Drucker, Chandler, Peters and Porter.

See also:

Miles, RE and Snow, CC (1978) *Organizational Strategy, Structure and Process*, McGraw-Hill, New York.
Simon, HA (1976) *Administrative Behaviour*, Macmillan, New York.

John Humble deserves a special mention as the person who brought management by objectives (MBO) to Britain (and, incidentally, whose thinking underpins some of the management approaches used formerly by Urwick Orr and, more recently, by Price Waterhouse). Although MBO was somewhat discredited because of bad design and over-rigid application, many of its principles still apply today. His main work is:

Humble, JW (1971) *Management By Objectives*, McGraw-Hill, Maidenhead.

Chapter 5   Organisation Design and Structure

The person who is credited with first establishing that an organisation's structure is linked to, and depends on, its strategy is Alfred Chandler. His most important work is probably:

Chandler, AD Jr (1962) *Strategy and Structure: Chapters in the History of the American Industrial Enterprise*, MIT Press, Cambridge, Mass.

Other key texts are:

Child, J (1984) *Organization: A Guide to Problems and Practice*, 2nd edition, Harper and Row, London.
Fayol, H (1949) *General Industrial Management*, Pitman, London.
Mintzberg, H (1979) *The Structuring of Organizations*, Prentice-Hall, New Jersey.
Mintzberg, H (1983) *Structures in Fives: Designing Effective Organizations*, Prentice-Hall, New Jersey.
Sloan, AP (1986) *My Years with General Motors*, Penguin, Harmondsworth.

Chapter 6   Jobs and Roles

On roles and role analysis:

Katz, D and Khan, RL (1966) *The Social Psychology of Organizations*, Wiley, New York.

Chapter 7   Teams and Groups

Some of the leading works are:

Argyris, C (1957) *Personality and Organization*, Harper and Row, New York.
Argyris, C (1964) *Integrating the Individual and the Organization*, Wiley, New York.

Descriptions of T-groups and encounter groups can be found in:

Blumberg, A and Golembiewski (1976) *Learning and Change in Groups*, Penguin, Harmondsworth.
Rogers, CR (1973) *Encounter Groups*, Penguin, Harmondsworth.

Probably the leading exponent of empowerment, as well as the de-layered post-entrepreneurial company, is Rosabeth Moss Kanter. Her best-known book is:

Kanter, RM (1989) *When Giants Learn to Dance*, Simon and Schuster, New York.

See also:

Belasco, JA (1992) *Teaching the Elephant to Dance*, Century, London.

Chapter 8   Motivation and Reward

Read:

McClelland, D (1961) *The Achieving Society*, Van Nostrand, New York.
Miner, JB (1980) *Theories of Organizational Behaviour*, Holt, Rinehart and Winston, San Diego, Ca.
Mitchell, TR (1982) *People in Organizations*, McGraw-Hill, New York.

...and just to prove that not all the names of writers on motivation begin with M, read the following on the Hawthorne experiments and Elton ... Mayo:

Roethlisberger, FJ and Dickson, WJ (1949) *Management and the Worker*, Harvard University Press, Harvard.

Chapter 9   The Management Role

Peters and Waterman, Tom Peters in particular, have become very well-known in recent years and are virtually required reading for anyone interested in management. Using the well-known McKinsey '7-S' formula (structure, strategy, systems, style of management, skills, staff and shared values) they analysed 43 successful companies and identified the following common characteristics:

- a bias for action;
- close to the customer;
- autonomy and entrepreneurship;
- productivity through people;

- hands-on, value driven;
- stick to the knitting;
- simple form, lean staff;
- simultaneous loose-tight properties.

In view of the relatively poor performance of many of the 'excellent' companies originally studied, the term was subsequently re-defined, referring now more to the ability to adapt to change. Major books are:

Peters, T and Waterman, RH Jr (1982) *In Search of Excellence*, Harper and Row, New York.
Peters, T and Austin, N (1986) *A Passion for Excellence*, Fontana, London.
Peters, T (1988) *Thriving on Chaos*, Macmillan, London.

From a study of chief executives, Mintzberg concluded that managerial work was characterised by '...brevity, variety and frag-mentation'. He also identified ten separate management roles: figurehead, leader, liaison, monitor, disseminator, spokesman, entrepreneur, disturbance handler, resource allocator and negotia-tor. These roles are subsumed or implied in the role descriptions in this chapter. See:

Mintzberg, H (1983) *The Nature of Managerial Work*, Harper and Row, New York.

Other relevant texts are:

Adair, J (1983) *Effective Leadership*, Pan Books, London.
Armstrong, M (1990) *How to Be an Even Better Manager*, Kogan Page, London.
Bennis, W and Nanus, B (1985) *Leaders: The Strategies for Taking Charge*, Harper and Row, New York.
Bennis, W (1989) *On Becoming a Leader*, Business Books, London.
Fiedler, FE (1967) *A Theory of Leadership Effectiveness*, McGraw-Hill, New York.
Pascale, RT (1990) *Managing on the Edge*, Viking, London.
Stewart, R (1967) *Managers and Their Jobs*, McGraw-Hill, Maidenhead.
Schonberger, RJ (1990) *Building a Chain of Customers*, Business Books, London.

Chapter 10   Communication

On report writing:

Gowers, E (1968) *The Complete Plain Words*, Penguin, Harmondsworth.

On personal interaction:

Honey, P (1976) *Face to Face: A Practical Guide to Interactive Skills*, IPM, London.

General:

Porter, LW and Roberts, KH (1977) *Communication in Organizations*, Penguin, Harmondsworth.
Stanton, N (1986) *What do you mean 'communication'?*, Pan, London.
Most books written by Greville Janner (for practical advice).

Index

self-actualisation needs 123, 124
service organisations
    matrix structures 78-80
    structure of 68
services
    differentiation of 68
    levels of 46
    and mission statements 50
    and organisation structure 67-8, 74
shaper, role in management team
    115
size
    as factor in comparison of
        organisations 23
    influence on organisation
        structure 69
social needs 122, 124
sociograms, and measurement of
    communication processes 43, 44
specialisation
    and organisation structure 65, 70
    of processes 69
    task 74, 96-7
staff turnover, statistical analysis of
    34
statistical analysis
    absenteeism and lateness 34
    employee attitudes 34-5
    grievance and disputes 34
    staff turnover 34
status, and barriers to
    communication 159-60
stereotypes
    as barrier to communication 160
    and dangers of group think 105,
        106
strategy
    acquisitions and mergers 58
    action planning 61-2
    balance of 59
    critical success factors (CSFs) 59-61
    development of 57-8
    financial criteria 59
    and internal consistency 59
    measurement of effectiveness 58-9
    and objectives 56-7
    and organisation structure 64, 65
    and personal values 59
    planning process 58
    risk factors 59
    and use of SWOT analysis 57-8
    see also management

stress
    and group formation 103
    and role conflict 93-5
structure *see* organisation structure
structure analysis
    job analysis 38-9
    organisation design criteria 35-7
supervision, and empowered teams
    117
supervisors
    power of 114
    role conflict and ambiguity 93-4,
        138
SWOT (Strengths, Weaknesses,
    Opportunities and Threats)
    analysis 29, 32
    and determining strategy 57-8
synergy, concept of, and company
    mergers 58
systems analysis, and process
    analysis 41

Tannenbaum, R and Schmidt, WH,
    on continuum of management
    styles 141-2
targets
    and bonus schemes 132
    and performance-related pay 131
    and timescales 139
task based job descriptions 88
task culture 47
task specialisation 74, 96-7
tasks
    and group effectiveness 108
    and leadership process 136-7
Taylor, FW, and scientific
    management 121-2
team worker, role in management
    team 116-17
team working, group technology
    approach 97
teams
    empowerment of 117-19
    ideal 114-17
    multi-functional 119
    relation of individual to 138-9
    see also groups
technology
    as factor in comparison of
        organisations 23
    and mission statements 50
    and organisation structure 70, 74,
        76